THE RIGHT TO RISE

*Bold Voices, Brave Journeys,
Unstoppable Spirits*

KAREN STRAUSS

Published by
Hybrid Global Publishing
333 E 14th Street #3C New York, NY 10003

Copyright © 2025 by Karen Strauss

All rights reserved. No part of this book may be reproduced or transmitted in any form or by any means, electronic or mechanical, including photocopying, recording, or by any information storage and retrieval system, without the written permission of the Publisher, except where permitted by law.

Manufactured in the United States of America, or in the United Kingdom when distributed elsewhere.

Strauss, Karen
The Right To Rise

ISBN: 978-1-938015-01-4 (Paperback)
ISBN: 978-1-957013-36-7 (E-book)

Cover design by: Julia Kuris
Copyediting by: Claudia Volkman
Book Interior and E-book design by: Amit Dey

Website: https://hybridglobalpublishing.com/

Disclaimer
The information provided in this book is intended for entertainment and general informational purposes. Some stories reference real individuals and companies, while others have been adapted, fictionalized or amalgamated to illustrate broader principles and ideas. Readers are advised to consult with a licensed professional before making any investment decisions. The author and publisher assume no liability for financial outcomes resulting from actions based on the content of this book.

CONTENTS

Foreword by Mark and Renee Porteous................v

Introduction by Karen Strauss....................ix

A Brain and Body You Can Trust in Midlife by Heather Awad . . 1

The Confession by Martina Chaconas................9

Joy by Anne Gordon..........................17

The Thresholds of Becoming by Marla Hall...........25

Rooted and Rising by Cynthia Haskins..............35

Staying Sane When Your World Goes Crazy by Rhetah Kwan. . 45

Cultivating Resilience—Letting Go, Letting In, Rising Strong
   by Karen Strauss..........................53

Misdiagnosis by Karen J. C. Sullivan, PhD...........61

Finding My Voice by Claudia Volkman..............69

Beyond the Pink: Awakening and Arising to a New Paradigm
   by Beverly Vote..........................75

Fire on the Front Lines: *Revolution versus the Flower Child Mirage*
   by Frances Whitten........................83

FOREWORD

There is a moment in every human journey when something deep within whispers: "You were made for more."

And if you're brave enough to listen ... that whisper becomes a roar.

The Right to Rise is a powerful echo of that call.

This book is a collective declaration of courage, resilience, and transformation. Each chapter is a lived testimony, a bold offering from someone who dared to rise beyond their struggle, who turned their pain into purpose, and who now lights the path for others.

These authors didn't wait until they had it all figured out. They didn't hide behind perfection or polish. They showed up with hearts wide open. Their stories are raw, real, and richly human. And in that, they are sacred.

We've seen the magic that happens when purpose-driven souls come together to share their truth. In 2021, we launched our first *Soulful Leadership* anthology with the unwavering support of Karen Strauss and Hybrid Global Publishing. Since then, we've co-created three bestselling books with transformational leaders who dared to speak from the soul. What began as a single ripple became a wave of collective empowerment, and we know the same is true here.

The Right to Rise isn't just a title. It's a birthright.

It speaks to something we all carry within us: a divine permission to rise, again and again, no matter what we've endured.

And it also speaks to responsibility. The more we rise, the more we're called to lift others. That's the beauty of a collaboration like this. It's not a solo ascent. It's a summit climbed together.

To the authors: your willingness to be seen, to tell the truth of your becoming, is what gives this book its power. You are not just telling stories. You are transmitting possibility. You are reminding the world that healing is real, transformation is available, and rising is always an option.

To the reader: This book found its way to you for a reason. These stories are mirrors. They will stir something inside you. You may laugh. You may cry. You may find yourself whispering, "Me too." And that's the invitation.

Let these words guide you home to the parts of yourself that are ready to rise.

Let them break something open in you.

Let them remind you: You are not alone. You are not broken. You are becoming.

We believe in your rise. We honor your path. And we welcome you into a community of leaders who grow, heal, and rise together.

With love and unwavering belief in what's possible,

—Mark and Renée Porteous

Co-founders of the Soul Affiliate Alliance and the Joint Venture Directory, **Mark and Renée Porteous** are dynamic duo-preneurs and conscious parents of twins, one girl and one boy.

Besides running the technology/operations side of their business, Renée owns and operates Divine Order Management, which supports transformational leaders with the day to day business operations, allowing them to focus on sharing their message with the world.

Known as "The Soul Connector," Mark is a joint venture strategist and affiliate concierge. Transformational leaders hire Mark to reach more people with their message by developing soulful alliances so they can make a greater impact in the world, while enjoying more freedom and ease.

Together, Mark and Renee are a powerful force, offering high-level guidance and connections, plus full management and technical support to leaders in the personal development industry.

markporteous.com

INTRODUCTION

A BOOK BORN IN A CIRCLE

This book didn't begin with a plan.
It began with a promise.

A promise we made to ourselves and to one another—to stop playing small. To stop waiting for the "right time" to use our voices. To finally share the stories we've carried, lived, and learned from.

The Right to Rise: Bold Voices, Brave Journeys, Unstoppable Spirits is the result of that promise.

Inside these pages are the voices of eleven women from the **Write to Rise Inner Circle**, a publishing mastermind that goes far beyond writing. We came together not just to create books—but to rise together in visibility, credibility, and purpose. We held each other through deadlines, self-doubt, breakthroughs, and bold declarations. And somewhere in that process, something beautiful happened:

We stopped trying to do it alone.

We didn't set out to write a "perfect" book. We set out to write an honest one.

You'll meet women who've navigated cancer, family secrets, spiritual awakenings, career pivots, and personal revolutions. But more than the stories themselves, you'll feel the thread that ties them together:

the willingness to be seen, not in spite of our wounds, but because of what we've learned from them.

This book was born in a circle—a space where we could write, reflect, and rise together. The **Write to Rise Inner Circle** gave us more than a structure for publishing; it gave us a community of women who held space for each other's voices, visions, and vulnerability.

This is what rising looks like—not alone, but in a circle.
A collective strength is woven through many stories.
And now that this book is in your hands,
you're part of that circle too.

Welcome in.

Karen Strauss
Publisher, Hybrid Global Publishing
Creator, Write to Rise Inner Circle
hybridglobalpublishing.com/innercircle

A BRAIN AND BODY YOU CAN TRUST IN MIDLIFE

Heather Awad

> *The feedback between mind and body is being replenished thousands of times a minute.*
>
> — *Deepak Chopra*

Nadia had given up on her body. A busy small business owner and well past menopause, she ate a mix of the healthy homemade Russian food she grew up with and American junk food. She hated her big tummy, but figured there was nothing to do about it. Routine bloodwork showed a high hemoglobin A1C: a marker that she was at risk for diabetes. She told her doctor she wanted to avoid medication if at all possible, and asked what she could do instead. "Lose weight!" her doctor said. Nadia hired me as her coach, and as we worked together, she learned to adjust her mindset and trust her body. She lost thirty pounds, but what she gained was even more valuable. Nadia now speaks kindly to herself and nourishes herself with healthy food. I have seen her in the years since that weight loss, and she continues to look and feel good. How did she do it?

Midlife is the time to find your kinder brain and reconnect with your body.

In Shirzad Chamine's book, *Positive Intelligence: Why Only 20% of People and Teams Achieve Their True Potential and How You Can Achieve Yours*, he describes the negative voice in our heads as "the Judge." At some point in childhood, he describes that we accept negative messages from important adults in our lives. "Most of us grow up experiencing love that is conditional on being good or performing, and we get into the habit of placing the same conditions on self-love". We weren't enough, we were stupid, we couldn't do things right. We were selfish, lazy, or not as good as that kid down the street. We were small and depended on those adults for our survival, so we accepted what they said to us. However, Shirzad points out that as adults, we no longer rely on our parents and teachers for food and shelter anymore, so we can also cast aside those views they expressed. Even though we have repeated this mean self-talk over and over, the phrases are merely thought loops in our brain that can be disrupted and shrunk. Those thought loops you hear in your brain are not you.

If you were going to do a 5K charity walk, you wouldn't wear your elementary school gym shoes. They don't fit anymore. Old negative thought loops don't fit either. I'm not talking about repeating fake positive mantras. Your brain knows those are false and will reject them. This is about talking to yourself like you would to a good friend. It's time to actually become a friend to yourself if you want to be successful at weight loss (and other big goals).

I spent a lot of time speaking harshly to myself during my first two years of medical school in order to motivate me to study hard. There were some really fun times in those first two years—parties at the medical frat house, talent shows, laughing with classmates over lunch—however, my overall memory of that time is that it was absolutely miserable. So even if you beat yourself up mentally to achieve a goal, you could choose a more encouraging and inspirational voice NOW for your weight loss journey or anything else you want to accomplish. Think of someone from your childhood such as a supportive parent, an inspirational teacher or coach, or a loving aunt or uncle, who might say something like this on a difficult day: "Wow, you had a rough day, but I know you can do it! You can get back out there tomorrow and make progress." If I could talk to my younger self, I would definitely tell her to find a positive and inspirational way to motivate herself through medical school.

Many women say, "I want to lose weight so I can feel good about myself again." These are separate and parallel tracks, but both are essential for lasting weight loss. The practical aspect of weight loss is mainly eating along menopause nutrition guidelines that work with your hormones, eating intentionally, and making plans on how you want to eat. Your weight loss journey is so much easier and enjoyable when you speak kindly to yourself. Since there is no thought police, you can choose to think anything you want. So choose thoughts that feel true, thoughts that your brain will accept. Here's how.

Using mean self-talk has the energy of pushing, forcing, flogging an exhausted horse. Speaking kindly to yourself has the energy of pulling, inspiring, inviting. Which energy do you want to be living in when you get to your goal weight? One of those energies will help you keep going forward in maintenance, while the other will hinder you. Here's an example: I once applied for a non-clinical doctor job at a tech start-up, and one of the doctors there said, "Working here is a lot like the first two years of medical school." Those were the miserable years I described earlier. I walked out and said no thank you to the job.

However, if you love yourself all the way through the process, you can easily keep going when you get to your goal weight. Can you see how this will allow you to go forward on your weight loss journey with ease?

Disrupt Negative Self-Talk

Here's an exercise I do with my clients. Write down a list of things that are great about you. See how many you can come up with. If you are having a hard time thinking of something, write down things nice things that others have said about you. They don't need to be serious, but they must be very complimentary. Some ideas:

- "That woman can really run an event."
- "Children love to hug you."
- "There's a badass radiologist."
- "Here is the dog whisperer."
- "You have nice hair."
- "Queen of the Electric Slide!"

Now, choose five things and write them on sticky notes. Place these on your bathroom mirror, where you'll see them when you get ready each day. When you notice that your brain wants to offer you some unkind personal remark about your appearance, instead, read out loud all five of the nice things about you. If your brain is still trying to say the mean phrase, just say hello to the Judge. "I hear you, and I'm not listening to you anymore."

How did that feel? Keep doing it every time you walk into that bathroom. You may find over time that you need to shuffle the notes around in a different formation to keep things fresh, but make sure you can still see your own face. You are making friends with her. Switch in some other sticky notes that sing your praises if needed, such as "You're the best broccoli maker!" "You are a loving daughter." "You have gorgeous eyes."

I must warn you, though—the Judge will fight back. You will walk by a living room mirror and suddenly you hear the Judge make a rude remark about your neck. Simply notice it and say, "I hear you

. . ." and then tell him to take a hike or say, "Are you trying to sneak up on me in the living room now, Judge?" These thought loops *can* be interrupted, and they *will* diminish. Little by little, the Judge will become an annoying fly that may come back from time to time, but the loving voice of yourself as a friend will take over.

Your Body Is a Luxury Vehicle

Midlife is the time to get serious about nourishing your body. I like to think of our bodies in the menopause transition and beyond as luxury vehicles. They need premium gas to run well. Regular gas, otherwise known the Standard American Diet (SAD) with lots of processed foods and unbalanced meals, will cause your menopause body to feel poorly. When you eat protein and vegetables or berries at a meal, notice if this helps you think better during the workday. Does making sure there are some healthy fats in that meal help you stay full longer?

Food and alcohol sensitivities often emerge at midlife. What are the things you used to eat without issue, that now cause stomach aches, headaches, or loose bowels? Take time to notice how foods make you feel. When you eat half a pizza, do you feel sleepy and dopey, or energetic and focused? How about when you eat two slices of pizza plus a side of roasted broccoli?

The Japanese have a phrase they say before eating: *Hara hachi bu*, meaning practice eating until you are 80 percent full. It's a mindful eating practice that sets the intention to eat moderately and not overeat. You leave a slight gap, where you feel satisfied but not full. This is a critical skill for living in a normal weight body.

Many of us have lost the ability to know how physical hunger truly feels. Physical hunger feels like a gnawing in your belly, and it comes and goes like waves. Your stomach might growl. If ignored, you may start to feel weak, lightheaded, and tired.

Sometimes you might feel an urgent hunger, but it doesn't fade in and out. This might be an emotional hunger. You may be feeling an emotion that you wish to change urgently, and food is one way to do that. See if you can name the emotion you are feeling, and identify where you feel it in your body. Is it across your forehead or a tightening in your shoulders? Is it an ache in your gut, or is it like squirrels running up and down your torso? Does it floats away like a cloud across the sky, or does it sit heavy on your shoulders and then slide away? Sometimes our emotions can point out something useful if we don't buffer them away with food:

- "I need to have a good talk with my teenager."
- "This supply problem will keep happening unless we put a monthly checks system in place."

If you are experiencing an uncomfortable emotion that doesn't fade away in a few minutes, you can change it quickly by stepping outside, turning on some music and dancing around, talking to a friend or colleague, or doing a deep breathing exercise. No junk food required!

The other situation that causes an urgent hunger is a blood sugar drop. If you don't have a hormone disease that causes low blood sugar, this is usually because you recently ate sugar or simple carbohydrates on their own. For example, if you eat puffed rice cereal with honey drizzled on top, you may feel hungry a couple of hours later. You can fix this with a little protein and fiber—like hummus and carrots—and remind yourself that you will likely want to choose a breakfast with protein and vegetables or berries tomorrow morning.

Your brain and body work together. Disrupting old thought loops of negative self-talk can help you meet goals, and they literally can change your outlook and improve the energy you take into your world. The menopause transition is a perfect time to start noticing how food makes us feel and how it affects our energy and concentration. It's also the ideal time to reconnect with the experience of physical hunger versus emotional hunger versus sugar withdrawal hunger. That way, we can fuel ourselves well so we can optimally run these excellent midlife bodies that carry us around. We will also be able to pay attention to our emotional hunger and needs, so we can give ourselves what will soothe us, support us, and solve problems, without the cheap, short-term fix of the wrong kinds of food.

Make friends with yourself. Smile at yourself in the mirror. Nourish your excellent, imperfect body and notice how good it feels. Midlife is the perfect time to trust your brain and body again.

Heather Awad, MD, is a family doctor and certified coach who helps professional women at the menopause transition and beyond to lose weight for the last time so they can live in the body they want. She hosts the *Vibrant Menopause* podcast, where she discusses weight loss and other midlife health topics.

vibrant-md.com

FREE GIFT from Heather Awad, MD:

Best Breakfasts for Menopause Weight Loss

Kickstart Weight Loss with the Right First Bite

The first meal of the day has a powerful impact on your hormones, cravings, and blood sugar all day. Get it right, and you're on your way to sustainable weight loss.

What's Inside?

- Doctor-approved breakfast ideas that help you stay full, focused, and satisfied all morning.
- Smart strategies for sweet tooth mornings—no sugar crash required.
- A simple, flexible breakfast formula designed to support menopause weight loss.

Vibrant-MD | Heather Awad, MD   www.vibrant-md.com/breakfast

THE CONFESSION

Martina Chaconas

"I guess I can tell you what happened now. The statute of limitations has expired, so they can't throw me in jail," my father casually remarked as we sat side by side on chaise lounges looking out onto the Mediterranean.

The sea was calm, its deep blue waters stretching out under the sun. The gentle waves caught the light like a polished stone. I had rendezvoused with my parents, my brother Michael, and his wife on the island of Cyprus. It was the summer after 9/11, and the world felt wounded to me. I didn't understand the level of hate and failure to accept our differences that had led to the murder of more than three thousand Americans. I needed to be with my family, to be in the presence of their tireless love and our collective understanding of just how fucking resilient we all are.

And frankly, I needed to laugh. The chatter of nearby tourists talking in their native tongues was soothing to me, even the guttural, rhythmic sounds of the German family lugging their gear to the water's edge. The smell of the sea had calmed my weary heart, or maybe it was just my father's presence.

Either way, he certainly had my attention.

I turned to him, not sure what he was about to confess. My father had been a former criminal defense lawyer in Washington, D.C., and there was a lot I witnessed as a child.

I held my breath, unsure of what was about to come spilling out. As I looked into his eyes, I realized they were the same loving eyes that stared back at me as a child with unconditional love and support, but they were clearly hiding something he had protected me from all these years.

Please, God, don't let this be the moment he tells me he had to kill or be killed. I wouldn't hold it against him, but this is the same man who raised me to scoop up spiders and rehome them outside rather than squash them out of fear.

"I'm responsible for stealing the Watergate Grand Jury transcripts and getting them to Jack Anderson, the syndicated columnist," he confessed.

And just like that I was taken back to our house on Welcome Drive in Falls Church, Virginia, sitting at the kitchen table doing my homework. On the wall behind the table was the poem by Dorothy Law Nolte, "Children Learn What They Live," with classic wisdoms like "When children live with honesty and fairness, they learn truth and justice," and "When children live with encouragement, they learn confidence." I must have read it a hundred times. I did my homework at this table, and the irony of studying most of my childhood in the shadow of this classic '70s poem is not lost on me. The gist of it was don't fuck up the kids, but it was already too late for that. I had experienced much too much tragedy—or shall I say "shifting circumstances"—for my tender age: two murders, a kidnapping, a rape, and watching someone take their last breath. I often read that poem and thought to myself, *We must have been cursed by a gypsy*; it was the only thing that made any sense to me.

It was at that table that I first asked my father about what happened at Watergate. We were studying it in Social Studies, and I was always interested in what my father had to say about history and government, but on that day all he said to me was, "Don't believe everything you read, kid," and walked out of the room." He didn't have to elaborate. I believed him and in my mind put a question mark next to Watergate.

Beyond the Swanson Salisbury Steak frozen meals laced with chemicals we would know nothing about for decades, the Ayds diet squares my mom washed down with Tab to stay slim, and the super-sugary Count Chocula cereal we ate, the 1970s were packed with so much drama and intrigue, at least in our home.

I remember one night when the phone rang at our house. Back in those days, it would ring incessantly until someone answered or simply took it off the hook. This particular night it had rung at least a dozen times, so I ended the torture and answered it. As the youngest member of the family, I usually never answered. I had better things to do like play with my Mrs. Beasley doll or practice a kick turn on my skateboard, but clearly everyone was too busy.

The husky voice on the other end of the line asked, "Is your father home?" As the child of a man who defended criminals for a living, I had learned early on to mind my answers and replied, "He's in the shower. Can I ask who's calling?"

There was a long silence. Then came his chilling response: "Tell him I'm coming to cut you all up."

Most kids would have freaked out at that, but we knew the drill. A wiry little tomboy, I jumped the first set of stairs to the front door landing below, then the second, and found my father making a cocktail at the bar in our wood-paneled rec room. As soon as I told him what the man said, he said, "Get the boys now." The look on his face told me he knew who it was and exactly what kind of violence might follow. In my mind, it involved a large knife of some kind.

That night my brother John was responsible for making sure the basement windows and the sliding doors were locked, one of which opened to a large yard that had no fence. Michael's job was to interrupt my sister's make-out session with her boyfriend, but I remember he kept watching TV. He couldn't handle the stress, still can't. I was perched at the infamous kitchen table on the second floor, watching the street. Even at night, the air hung heavy with moisture, clinging to my skin. My legs stuck to the thick clear plastic that covered the turquoise-colored cushion of the chair for what felt like an eternity. I was too afraid to shift to Indian-style, in case I missed anything while adjusting my legs.

It would all come to an end soon enough.

William Patrick Covington, the man on his way to our house, had been found guilty of robbing a bank with his partner, Sal Lucero. He was sentenced to twenty-five years in state prison. A former client of my father's, Covington was known to be a brutally violent man. My father refused to speak about it, even to my mother, but we understood that Covington meant what he said. I can still hear his voice in my head, calm, resolute.

That night, on his way to our house, he murdered a young woman and took her car. He had escaped from prison and had one thing on his mind: vengeance. He blamed my father for not getting him off, as so many of the guilty did.

We had no idea where Covington was when he made that call, but we couldn't take any chances that he'd catch us off guard. The six of us were all seated at the kitchen table, chairs lined up and facing the double-casement windows, waiting. No one said a word. We knew that if our father was silent, this was a bona fide threat.

Our house on Welcome Drive sat across the street from a wooded patch concealed a large municipal water tank. The only thing visible in the shadows was the red ember glowing from the end of a cigarette.

If it was Covington, what was he waiting for?

I used to watch *Perry Mason* episodes with my father. It was our thing. He'd recline in my grandfather's Barcalounger, and I'd lie on the brown shag carpet, listening to every word Perry uttered. I loved what I knew of the law at a young age—that justice must be served. I truly believed I would grow up to follow in my father's footsteps, but fate had something different in mind for me, something that didn't involve violent criminals.

Moments after the shadowy figure tossed his cigarette on the ground and began crossing the street toward our house, an unmarked Plymouth Fury pulled up. Two men wearing dark suits exited the car and grabbed the man. There was a number my father would call whenever he received credible threats like this. That was the last I saw of William Patrick Covington, bank robber and soon-to-be convicted murderer.

Years later, John told me a story about how our father answered the front door wearing nothing but a white T-shirt and Bermuda shorts. He left, shoeless, with a man John didn't recognize. John was a secretive kid and only told me the story when I was sixteen, because I desperately wanted to buy a Volkswagen Karmann Ghia, and my father, always so easygoing, would not let me have one.

"What's so wrong with a Volkswagen?"

"I said no. Absolutely not, and that's all I'll say on the matter."

He offered no explanation for why he forbade it. I would learn years later that the man at the front door, another client, had taken him at gunpoint in a Karmann Ghia to West Virginia to kill him and dump his body in one of the expansive wooded areas, a pre-dug grave waiting for him. Fortunately, my father wrestled the gun away from the man. This is why he would never let me have that car, clearly a memory he didn't want to be reminded of.

"No" was not a word my father said often. His love language was any way he could be agreeable. My brother John totaled three cars in high school. The fact that our father gave him another after he crashed the first one is hard to fathom, let alone two.

John was the first child my parents had together; both had been married before and met as divorcés. My mother worked at the World Bank in Washington, D.C., as an executive assistant, and she modeled to make extra cash to care for my sister Paula—mostly for department stores like Lord & Taylor and Neiman Marcus. One of her friends, another model who happened to be Greek as well, invited her to a party at Nick Chaconas' house.

My mother was the kind of woman who walked into a room and people stopped what they were doing just to take her in. She had been a stand-in for Sophia Loren when Loren was shooting the Paramount film *Houseboat* with Cary Grant. They filmed around Washington, D.C., Maryland, and Virginia, and when my mother showed up to the casting call, the search was over. They had discovered the Greek version of Sophia.

After the shooting wrapped up, they asked her to come to Los Angeles to do a screen test, but she politely declined and told the producer that her daughter was her priority. That was only part of the story, though. Sophia was quite harsh to her, and one day in particular brought my mother to tears. Cary Grant, always the gentleman, consoled her, telling her, "Darling Lydia, you must understand that Sophia is used to being the only beautiful woman on set." He squeezed her hands, kissed her cheek, and instantly erased any damage that had been done.

Evangeline "Lydia" Agius emigrated to America when she was eighteen. She had been sponsored by Craig Starbuck Atkins, an American judge she met in Athens. The Judge, as he was nicknamed, asked my Papou (grandfather) if he could bring my mother to America, and my Papou agreed. Both men may have had ulterior motives: the Judge wanted to introduce her to his eligible son, and my Papou may have been trying to avoid paying a dowry to her future groom.

I don't pretend to understand what it's like to survive a World War. To be forced out of your home, fleeing in the night with no plan, driven only by the desire to stay alive. I choose to believe that's what guided my Papou when he entrusted his beloved daughter to a man he barely knew, sending her across the world without family. He wanted her somewhere safe, far from the devastation and the memories of barely escaping the Germans, who, in their cruelty, might have claimed my mom for themselves.

Sitting on the chaise beside my father, I reflected on his words and had my own confession. I realize I am the beautifully fucked-up product of both of their journeys—a man who stood by his principles, even when it brought hardship, and a woman whose courage showed in her faith in others, even when that trust was misplaced. Both are incredibly resilient, as am I.

Martina Chaconas has survived three decades in the advertising business as a creative director. Her debut book, *The Imperfect Patriot*, is the story of her tumultuous upbringing and her father's role in the Watergate scandal. She lives in Los Angeles with her partner of twenty-five years, Jennice, their son, Jasper, and both of her nonagenarian parents, Pete and Lydia.

The Imperfect Patriot

Scan the QR code to watch my
interview with the
Imperfect Patriot himself

JOY

Anne Gordon

> *The body heals with play, the mind heals with laughter, and the spirit heals with joy.*
>
> —*Proverb*

It is impossible not to smile when you see a dolphin!

You can feel the joy the dolphins bring even in a photo or video. It's fascinating to watch people on whale-watching tours when dolphins show up. I've seen them go from quiet and hopeful to animated and excited with broad smiles on their faces. I watched one day as a man burst into song as the dolphins were gliding effortlessly in front of the boat.

The dolphins shared with me the reason we instantly feel joy when we see them:

When we ride the bow waves of your boats it is fun for us, but more importantly, we are surrounding and immersing you with our joy, love and healing energy.

Dolphins are the masters of joy. Their mission on Earth is to help us reconnect to joy. In our busy lives, it's easy to forget about joy. Sometimes we put joy into the category of someday, hoping to feel joy again like we did as children when joy was a constant presence in our lives.

Horace Dobbs, PhD, took clinically depressed people to swim with wild dolphins, and after just one swim they came out functional! People who suffered from chronic depression, who could not hold a job, have a romantic relationship, or even live on their own were able to find work, start dating, and get an apartment after swimming with dolphins.

Bill Bowell went with Dr. Dobbs to swim with a dolphin, and he explains what happened:

> I was a recluse, paranoid, aggressive and suffered from self-loathing. My life changed forever when I swam with a dolphin. He looked straight into my eyes for a few minutes, and I burst into tears. I was mesmerized and all my emotions erupted like a volcano. He nudged my face and tickled my ribs until I laughed out loud. My wife said it was the first time she had seen me smile in a year. Now, I take no medication and have returned to work. I am finally able to talk to my children again after almost ten years of barely knowing who they were.

That is the power of joy and the power of spending time with dolphins.

Joy Is a Choice

The dolphins have taught me so much about joy, but the most important thing they have shared with me is that joy is a choice. It is meant to be a permanent state, unlike fleeting emotions like happiness, sadness, or frustration that come and go quickly through us.

It is easy to be in joy, always. It is a simple choice. You make a decision to be in joy and you will be. It is as simple as that.

For some reason humans spend most of their time focused on negative thoughts, sadness, what they are worried about or afraid of. What does that bring you? More negativity, sadness and fear.

By choosing to be in joy, then life brings you more things to be joyful about. Life feels easy, fun and in the flow.

We watch you humans struggle and suffer so much. We try to bring you joy and it works when you see us. But the minute you step off the boat or away from the beach, you allow all your negative thoughts to come flooding back in.

What if you could feel as joyful as you do when you are with us every day, all day long? You can. Just choose joy. Let the negative thoughts flow back out of you as fast as they flow in.

There is always something in your life to be joyful about. Your love of us, your friends, your family, your talents, your love of yourself, your pets, your favorite shirt, a good book, food in your tummy, a warm shower, the list is endless.

When you feel the negative thoughts flowing in, just ignore them and write or make a mental list of everything you have in your life right now to be joyful about. You will feel the joy in no time.

Make a game out of finding things to be joyful about. That's what we do. We can find joy no matter what is happening around us, even in the face of danger. We feel joy for our physical and mental abilities, the adrenaline rush that heightens our senses and makes us feel alive. For being able to move past the danger to resume our normal activities. You can do the same when you come face to face with life's challenges.

The whales also have much to say about choosing joy. For instance:

Humans think life is a series of problems. It is not. Life is a series of experiences, and it is up to you to choose how to feel and react.

Life Is a School of Joy

What if we saw all the experiences we have in life as a way to teach us joy? Listen to what the dolphins have to say:

If each of you could learn not to take life so seriously and see your life for the school of Joy it truly is. That each hurdle you confront and surpass is one step closer to Mastery and Nirvana.

We are always smiling, even through our grief and frustration. Joy is our baseline emotion. Feeling emotions are the gift of having a physical body. In spirit one does not feel extreme emotions like here on Earth. In our bodies we rejoice when we experience the highs and lows of all emotions. It reminds us of the gift of our physical bodies and all we can do with them. When we feel our emotions we feel alive in a way that cannot be experienced as spirit.

Even in the Midst of Grief...

Years ago I was preparing to lead my first Dolphin Bliss in Bimini Retreat. It was my biggest group ever: twenty people swimming with wild dolphins on the tiny island of Bimini in The Bahamas. At the time, I was living in Panama and was married to an indigenous man from the Emberá tribe, who still live in traditional villages deep in the rainforest.

My husband's mother, Agricia, had become a dear friend with whom I always loved spending time. We loved sitting together, telling each other stories about our very different lives.

A few months prior to leaving for my retreat, Agricia had started having pains in her stomach. She saw several doctors, but they could never find any cause for the pain and sent her home each time. She would rally and seem fine, but then a few weeks later the pain would come back. It was frustrating for us all, but none of us thought it was anything serious since the doctors always sent her home.

I flew to the US a few days before my retreat to attend a business networking event, and Agricia seemed to be doing better. While I was at the event, though, I received a text from my brother-in-law that said, "My mother left us." My first thought was *Where did she go?*—which is what I texted back. He responded with "She died."

What? I called my husband immediately, and he confirmed that his mother had passed away. I was in shock and saddened that I was thousands of miles away and could not be there to grieve and support him and the rest of his family.

I heard this very sad news on a Friday, and on Sunday, I had to welcome all twenty participants who were traveling from all over the world to swim with the dolphins and learn dolphin wisdom from me. All I wanted to do was cry and jump on a flight back to Panama. My husband reassured me that he and his family were fine without me. I was also committed to being there for those who had signed up to spend a week with me and the dolphins, so I reluctantly continued with my plans.

On Sunday afternoon I put on my best happy face and went to greet my group of excited retreat participants. I was able keep my emotions in check until Tuesday morning, the day of the funeral. I spoke to my husband just before we went out on the boat to find the dolphins.

I realized there was no way I could hold back my tears, so I decided to share with my group about my mother-in-law's untimely passing and that today I was missing her funeral. I also shared what the dolphins had taught me about joy—that it is a choice and a permanent state. I explained that while I was sad, I was also in a state of joy to be on a catamaran sailboat in this tropical location surrounded by the most gorgeous turquoise blue water anywhere and sharing it with all of the amazing people who came to be on my retreat.

Two of the ladies in my group thanked me for sharing my grief with them as they had each lost someone very important to them in the last year and neither had given themselves permission to grieve the loss. They were deeply moved by my story and the idea that you can grieve and be in joy at the same time.

That day turned out to be our best dolphin encounter of the whole week. We found a pod of about forty Atlantic Spotted dolphins who came to our boat and welcomed us into the water to swim with them. They were so generous and gracious, staying with us for what felt like hours. Everyone got in the water—even one older man who walked with a cane and a woman who was afraid of the water. Every single person had an incredible, up close and personal experience with the dolphins. It was the encounter they had hoped and dreamed for when they signed up for the retreat.

I got in the water, too, but hung back from the group. I was still feeling sad, and I was perfectly happy to stay in the periphery and watch everyone else having such magical moments with the dolphins.

But one dolphin had a different idea. She swam up to me, stopped, and looked me directly in the eyes. Then she started swimming slow circles around me, which meant that to keep eye contact with her, I had to spin my body in circles to follow her. She swam around me four or five times until I couldn't help but burst out laughing in my mask and snorkel (which is not easy to do!). When I started laughing, the dolphin stopped. She looked me deep in my eye, as if to say, "My job here is done," and then she swam off.

Clearly, I was not meant to be just an observer that day. Dolphins are all about community and keeping the pod together, and this dolphin knew exactly what I needed: to laugh even while feeling sad and to give me a perfect illustration for how joy is always within us and can easily be brought to the surface even during times of great sadness.

A Message from the Atlantic Spotted Dolphins on Joy

Joy! Joy! Joy! We are the bringers of Joy. More so than any other species of dolphin. We embody pure Joy.

We are the welcoming committee. We open your heart with our playful antics. We love to interact with you and envelope you into our pod. Our greatest joy is watching you recapture your inner joy when you are with us.

Swimming with us brings you back to your natural state. The state of being you were in when you were born. Before anything bad ever happened to you. Your natural state of being is Joy.

When you were born you came into this life remembering the Bliss and Joy of being Spirit, of living in a higher dimension alongside the angels, where this is nothing but Joy and Love. Swimming with us brings you right back to this incredible feeling that you were born with.

With so much fear and anger in your world these days, it is so very important and healing for you, and the entire world, to step back into Joy.

Spending time with us will allow you not only to remember your Joy, but will give you a renewed sense of confidence to return to your life inspired to share this Joy with the world. When you leave you will inspire others to find their own Joy as well.

Choose Joy

Life is meant to be enjoyed. It is right there in the word, en-joy, *in joy. It is very simple. Stop making life so complicated. Choose Joy. Enjoy!*

It really is that simple. How can you bring more joy into your life? Start a Joy Journal and write down everything that brings you back to joy.

Anne Gordon is an experienced retreat leader, spiritual mentor, and founder of the Dolphin~Whale Energy Healer Certification Program. Using a unique blend of oceanic wisdom and practical guidance, her work supports energy healers, coaches, and spiritually minded individuals in expanding their impact, deepening their intuitive gifts, building purpose-driven, heart-led lives, and aligning with their highest potential.

whaleanddolphinwisdomretreats.com

You have your very own personal Dolphin Spirit Guide that has been with you since birth, watching over you, supporting, protecting and loving you. In this free, downloadable meditation led by Anne Gordon, you will meet your Dolphin Spirit Guide and create a lifelong relationship to receive personal insights, messages and healing just for you.

THE THRESHOLDS OF BECOMING

Marla Hall

> *No threshold need be a threat, but rather an invitation and a promise.*
>
> — John O'Donohue, "Thresholds"

There was a time I thought I knew who I was—because I had a job title, a schedule, a rhythm. I didn't have a master plan. I moved with the shifting trade winds of life, shaping days as they came. But I would learn that thresholds don't announce themselves. They arrive disguised as disruptions, inviting us to cross from who we were into who we're becoming.

Threshold One: The Six-Month Silence

It was supposed to be temporary—just a medical leave. A few weeks off work to recover. But weeks became six months. At first, I welcomed it. I slept in. I decluttered the house. I donated bags of what no longer fit. But when the drawers were clean and the silence settled in, I realized something terrifying: I didn't know how to live without a to-do list.

Without the structure of work, I was lost. The days stretched long and formless. Time slowed to a crawl. Meaning scattered like leaves in the wind.

And then, one Sunday morning, I noticed something that had always been there—the event listings in the newspaper. It became my roadmap. I began showing up: museum lectures, classes at Everywoman's Village, gatherings of strangers who would become guides. I built a life from curiosity. I re-learned joy. And unknowingly, I rehearsed "RetireMEANT" long before I had the language for it.

After three months on leave, I was told I would no longer be able to return to the position I had grown to love—but I was guaranteed another job. I grieved the loss of that role, felt happy for the person who would now own it, and tried to ready myself for whatever was coming.

Your Turn: Think of a time when a familiar structure or daily routine disappeared from your life. What emotions surfaced for you in that emptiness. Did you notice new possibilities, or did you feel lost at first? What did you discover about yourself? Was there something unexpected that guided you forward?

Threshold Two: Seeds Beneath the Surface

The seeds of RetireMEANT were already planted during that stretch of time off work—though I didn't yet know it. It had to do with the quiet that came after the initial action steps. When the novelty of freedom wore off, something deeper stirred.

I found myself sitting with the very questions so many face later in life: Where do I go from here? What gives my life meaning now? I didn't have the language yet, but I had the feeling—that ache that pulses at the edge of purpose. That's where it began, not in awareness, but in longing. Silently taking root, it would remain underground for the next thirty-five years.

Your Turn: What questions or longings have surfaced for you during times of change or loss? Is there an "ache" or curiosity that's nudged you toward something new? What might these questions be inviting you to explore or become?

Threshold Three: The Return That Broke Everything Open

What came with the return to work was a seismic change. The department had relocated from a place I could easily drive to; I now had to travel to downtown Los Angeles. This was before subways, so I had to park my car in a park 'n ride lot and travel by bus to my new office. My new commute consumed three hours a day, and what had once been passion now felt like burden.

I stayed for a couple of months. But the thrill, the challenge, the stimulation of my previous role were gone. The workflow no longer offered learning, testing, or meaningful interaction. Downtown Los Angeles back then was far from beautiful, but it bubbled with excitement—new places to discover. Still, that energy couldn't compensate for eight hours of disconnection followed by a grueling commute.

So, I quit.

No plan. No job. No preparation.

Just a raw inner knowing: *This isn't it.*

Your Turn: Have you ever walked away from something without a plan, simply because you knew it wasn't right? What was that leap of faith moment like for you? What gave you the courage to step into the unknown? What did you learn from the experience?

Threshold Four: The Bridge of Becoming

I went back to school—first for an associate's degree, then a bachelor's degree in rehabilitation counseling, and finally a master's degree. My earlier work became a bridge—not just to new jobs, but to a new way of seeing myself. I wasn't just preparing for work. I was preparing for something bigger.

Once again, my past experiences—employment, education, and life navigation—formed the skill sets I would carry into new expressions. This is what I tell the people I work with now: Your lived experience isn't over when a role ends. It's evolving. It's waiting for a new context.

Your Turn: What past experiences or skills have unexpectedly become new bridges to new opportunities in your life?

Threshold Five: The Door That Waited

After graduating with my master's in marriage, family, and child counseling, I was ready to seek employment. During my college years, I had worked for a psychologist who managed a Rational Emotive Therapy (RET) Center. But in a strange twist of timing, the Center closed just as I completed my degree. Once again, I was cast into uncertainty—and once again, a temp job became my unexpected lifeline.

Though I never formally worked in the field of counseling, my bachelor's degree in rehabilitation counseling and my early experience in emerging IT systems opened a door: a temporary role in a Worker's Compensation Department that would eventually evolve into the foundation of my thirty-year career.

Your Turn: Have you ever found yourself at a closed door, only to discover another one opening unexpectedly? What did you learn from that detour?

Threshold Six: The Vacation That Cracked Me Open

Twenty years later, on the Friday before a vacation to Montreal and Quebec, I was called into my supervisor's office. The presence of Human Resources told me everything: Unemployment awaited me. Two others in my division also were called in to hear their fate—part of a quiet and unsettling shift that carried its own unspoken weight.

The others had titles, authority, and seniority. I had none of those.

But I had something else: the Universe aligned with my highest and best. I didn't have practiced resilience—I had a divine architecture forming beneath the surface. It became a plan that served as the foundational connection to my next threshold, one I never saw coming. I had an invisible soul partner called synchronicity who always showed up at the right time, silently preparing me for the next chapter.

While I was away, a message on my work phone signaled a potential transfer. Until that call, I had worn a vacation mask—gleeful, excited, eager and ready to explore. But that call cracked something open. I finally shared my angst and worry, even though nothing was yet certain. I knew I'd have to wait until Monday to speak with anyone—and so I began quietly mapping out next steps, imagining who else to speak with, building a bridge I hadn't expected to need.

I had no sense of what would unfold—only a hope that saying yes would be enough for now.

I didn't know then that this transfer—this pivot—wasn't an exit. It was the entry point into something larger. It was the beginning of my next threshold.

Your Turn: When has an unexpected disruption or loss turned out to be the doorway to something better? What invisible architecture has supported you through change?

Threshold Seven: The Loan That Became a Lifeline

Sometimes detours become destinations. Another synchronicity was at work—I just didn't know it yet, much like the start of my career with this company.

The following Monday, I showed up excited and ready to begin working in my new position in my new department and new division. I met my new co-workers. And, then to my surprise,

I found out that I wouldn't start working in it immediately. It seemed that this position that I was meant to fill was still occupied by a temporary employee who had three months left on his contract.

So, they loaned me out to another department that could use my background and expertise. That temporary assignment would become the thread that wove itself back into my story.

Eventually, I returned to my new department and enjoyed eleven years in my new role. When you work for an entertainment company, you don't think about retirement—that is until you attend an All Hands Meeting and find out your department is being outsourced. Four months later, the international handoff was finalized. The work was rerouted, and we, the employees, were officially terminated.

Your Turn: Recall a time when your path took an unexpected detour. What did you learn? What gifts did this detour bring you— even if you only recognized their value much later?

Threshold Eight: When Endings Circle Back as Beginnings

It could have felt like an ending.

But something in me had already begun preparing for what might come next.

Without telling anyone, I had enrolled in a Quality Assurance IT Application Testing course. Quietly, I studied. Quietly, I earned my certification.

The day after I received the certification, the phone rang.

It was my former company.

They were looking for a consultant—someone to serve as a liaison between the stakeholder I had once supported and the division now carrying their work. The users—accustomed to first-class customer service—weren't feeling comfortable with the new team. They needed someone who understood both their system and the new support structure. Someone who could build the trust bridge between what was and what would be.

It turned out the department I had been loaned to for those three months was now calling me back.

I consulted with them for two years.

And when the goal was met—when I had done what I came to do—I left. Not in search of what was next, but in deep trust that what I had built would remain.

Another threshold had closed.

And something else was stirring—something that needed a few more years to rise: Retire On Fire, my new brand.

Your Turn: When has an ending in your life unexpectedly led to a new beginning. What signs or "nudges" helped you recognize that a new chapter was taking shape? What did you learn about yourself in that process?

Threshold Nine: The Ongoing Becoming

RetireMEANT didn't begin when I left work.

It began in these thresholds—each one an initiation into a deeper truth.

I had learned that your role can be taken, your job can be outsourced, your plans can be rerouted—but your essence? Your essence remains.

And when you listen to the still, small whisper within, that essence will always guide you home.

What I didn't know in 1973, in that Threshold of Silence, was that I wasn't just facing a career shift—I was rehearsing for the message I now carry. Meaning, expression, adventure, nurturing, and transformation aren't optional extras in RetireMEANT. They are essential ingredients in any life that still wants to burn bright.

This is not a story about endings.

It's a story about remembering.

About saying yes to the unexpected classroom.

About meeting the mess and finding your message inside it.

I am still becoming.

Still uncovering.

Still rewriting the definitions of purpose, of work, of value, of visibility. But now I walk with a roadmap—the one I lived into, not the one I planned. And this time, I'm not hiding in the shadows.

I am on fire with RetireMEANT.

Your Turn: Are you lost in retirement's "time freedom maze," asking, "Who am I now?" and "What's my purpose?" What part of you remains unchanged, no matter what roles or titles come and go? Where do you hear your own still, small whisper? That is your very own MEANT awaiting your discovery!

 For eighty-one-year-old **Marla Hall**, retirement is a launchpad, not a finish line. As a RetireMEANT Lifestyle Strategist, she guides others toward their own "MEANT (meaning, expression, adventure, nurturing, transformation) to do, be, have" evolution. Marla personifies this, as she is now completing a PhD in metaphysics she began in 1976.

Retire On Fire - Purpose Passion Possibilities | Facebook

ROOTED AND RISING

Cynthia Haskins

We all eat. Every single one of us.

And yet, in the very industries that feed the world, women are still fighting for equal ground. From sales and marketing to culinary innovation, food manufacturing, and grocery retail, women have always been part of the story, but too often, we've been cast as supporting characters. Only a few have made it into leadership roles.

I've spent more than four decades in the food industry, primarily in sales and marketing. I've stood at trade show booths, walked warehouses, met with buyers, pitched programs, built brands, and navigated boardrooms where leadership rarely looked like me. I've seen firsthand how much influence women have in food and how few are invited to the tables where decisions are made.

Over the years, the number of women moving into leadership roles has grown, and strides have been made in closing the wage gap. Still, we have a long way to go. According to the U.S. Census Bureau, in 2023, women working full-time earned 17 percent less than their male counterparts. In food service, an industry where women dominate the labor force, fewer than one in five hold executive chef roles. Across the food supply chain, male leadership remains the default. And yet, women are responsible for 70 to 80 percent of household food purchases.

Women drive demand. We shape trends. We feed the next generation. We're the ones being marketed to, yet too often we're missing from the teams making the decisions that affect our food system. This isn't just unfair—it's inefficient. It's outdated. And it's time we call it what it is: a missed opportunity.

Women have always been at the center of the table. Now it's time we take our rightful place at the table.

Rooted in Purpose

I was maybe five or six the first time I sat with my mother and older sister in the backyard, aprons tied, a colander between us and a bushel of green beans waiting to be snapped. We didn't talk much; it was just the rhythmic *snap, snap, snap* of breaking beans, the rustle of aprons, and the occasional quiet chat.

At the time, I didn't know we were doing anything special. But those afternoons shaped who I would become.

We were participating in a quiet ritual, one passed down through generations of women who've fed their families by gathering, preparing, and nourishing. Women who've carried more than their share of invisible labor. This was a gathering. A knowing. A way of being that didn't need to be spoken. We understood the place that had been made for us.

We lived on a small fruit and vegetable farm in northern Illinois. My father had moved us across the country to follow his dream of owning land. He worked nights at the railroad and during the day, he did the planting with us kids alongside him. My mother handled everything else: raising five children, pulling weeds, tending the garden, harvesting produce, and running the heart of our roadside stand.

She was a quiet woman who led by presence. She showed me how to carefully place the tomatoes so they wouldn't bruise. She wiped cucumbers clean and laid them out with the price written on handwritten signs. She peeled back just enough husk on the sweet corn so customers could peek inside, but not enough to dry it out. She never said she was teaching me anything, but I was learning everything.

I especially loved snapping green beans with her. I'd tie the apron around my little waist, proud to help. We'd sit in silence, our hands busy, the shade trees keeping us cool. Her hands were always moving—never rushed but always sure. That time in the backyard was sacred. Solid. Home. And though I couldn't name it then, I felt it: I belonged to something bigger.

The Gatherers

Across the South, and in small towns all over the country and the world, women have gathered like this for decades. Snapping beans. Shelling peas. Canning tomatoes. It's never just about food. It's about presence. It's about the quiet transfer of gathering, story, and purpose.

The backyard under the weeping willow became my first boardroom. My first classroom. My first circle of women.

And though I didn't know it yet, I was learning something I would carry with me for life: that food connects us. That women carry systems on their shoulders and rarely get credit. And that some of the most powerful leadership traits don't speak loudly but snap in rhythm and build legacy—one handful of green beans at a time.

I didn't know there was a whole world waiting for me. I had never been outside our little town with its one grocery store, a post office, and a single church. But I knew, even then, that my passion for agriculture ran deep.

I didn't know what I wanted to be. I didn't know what I was allowed to imagine. But I knew this: I wanted to contribute and be part of something. At that time, it was simply about planting the seeds and arranging the fresh produce just right so customers would line up around the block to buy.

And that was the beginning of everything.

Where Roots Begin

What I didn't realize as a little girl snapping green beans was that I was being trained in more than just domestic rituals; I was being shaped by a model of leadership that rarely gets recognized. My mother never asked for applause, never led with a title or a business card, but everything around her moved in quiet rhythm because of her. She made decisions, managed operations, solved problems, and kept everything running without ever calling it leadership. And yet, that's exactly what it was.

This early exposure to food, farming, and the roles women play within both reveals how deeply embedded gender expectations are in our cultural systems. In that backyard, I learned that food is more than nourishment. It's identity. It's care. It's work. And as I carved out a career around food, I began to understand that women's contributions, especially in agriculture and food systems, are often undervalued, even when they are essential.

The labor women perform in the background—from gardens to kitchens to roadside stands—sustained families and communities for years. From the sidelines of every restaurant, every food manufacturer, and every grocery store, there are unsung heroes. These invisible roles formed the very foundation of the food industry. But because they happen quietly, they have been, and still are, overlooked in boardrooms, budgets, and leadership structures.

The story of food is the story of women. And if we want to create a more equitable society, we must start by rewriting how we define contribution, whom we credit, and where we look for wisdom. Because real leadership isn't always loud. Sometimes, it sounds just like a green bean snapping in the hands of a five-year-old girl, learning what it means to matter.

A Different Kind of Garden

What began in the backyard was more than a childhood memory. It was the start of my education in care, patience, and quiet strength. Years later, I carried those same values into a much different kind of garden: the corporate world. But unlike the backyard, the air wasn't warm with comfort. It was thick with preconceived ideas about a woman's place.

I still remember my first big sales call in the produce industry. I was nervous and hopeful, manila folder prepared, suit freshly pressed, heels clicking toward possibility as I entered one of the wholesaler's facilities. Semitrucks lined up in front of the dock, unloading and reloading pallets of fresh produce for stores and restaurants.

Then a husky voice called out:
"Can I help you, little lady?"

"I'm here to see Todd," I replied.

He pointed toward the office.

The room smelled stale. A beam of light cut through the dirty window. Posters hung from aging tape. I stepped in, careful not to trip over a vacuum cord. Two chairs, both taken by jackets. I wondered if I was just supposed to stand there. I felt awkward. I was awkward.

"Hi, I'm Cynthia," I said.

He folded his arms.

"I'm here to talk about setting up some promotions."

"That's a good place for you," he said.

"In marketing?" I clarified.

"No. Next to the vacuum cleaner," he said.

And I laughed.

Not because it was funny, but because I'd been conditioned to laugh during moments like this. Conditioned, like a rose trained to climb a wall, to twist myself into something palatable, nonthreatening, agreeable, polite. That brittle, reflexive laugh was a way to protect pride, even as it cost me a piece of myself.

That experience wasn't just about one man. It was about a system. An entire industry where women were expected to be presentable but invisible. Skilled but not outspoken. Ambitious, but not too much.

One Leaf at a Time

That story is more than just an uncomfortable anecdote. It's a reflection of how women in male-dominated industries are trained, often unconsciously, to adapt, shrink, and absorb discomfort just to stay.

These structures that have existed for decades—and still do. The irony is that women bring incredible value to the food industry. We're strategic thinkers, empathetic leaders, creative problem-solvers.

Yet we spend more energy navigating culture than doing the work we're more than capable of doing.

When women aren't given real seats at the table, the industry loses insight, innovation, and inclusion. When our presence is merely tolerated, we're forced to choose between being accepted or being authentic. But safety isn't the same as belonging. And belonging is what creates growth.

That moment in the office was the beginning of my awareness and my resolve. I stayed. I adapted. I succeeded. And eventually, I began to plant something different: not just roots of resilience, but roots of change.

If you're a woman working in agriculture or the food industry, you have more power than you know to name what isn't right, to ask for what you need, and to open doors for others. The systems may still resist, but we don't have to prune ourselves to fit anymore.

The Garden Within

Every one of us has a gift. But too often, we don't fully recognize it, let alone believe in it. The key is learning how to be still long enough to hear our inner voice, listen to what our deeper selves are trying to unfold, and give our dreams room to bloom.

The best and biggest investment we can make is within ourselves. That is the root of everything. And we don't have to do it alone. There are millions of women across the country and around the world who know, deep inside, that we are worthy of our rightful place—even if that worth has been tucked away to stay protected.

Our worthiness has been dormant. Now it's time to bear fruit and let that fruit multiply. It's time to join the millions of other women seeking equal ground. Meet others in workshops, conferences, and online communities.

It can be scary to go out on a limb for yourself, fearing it might break beneath you. But you have a whole sector of women behind you. Invest in yourself. Read books. Listen to podcasts. Watch videos that fuel your growth. Seek out opportunities. Ask for the promotion. Begin that business. Show up for yourself.

Dig deep and discover what you believe is holding you back. Name it. Then begin the work of healing it. We usually know what holds us back, and it takes courage to unveil it, even to ourselves. But when you do, something powerful happens. What once felt impossible begins to feel inevitable. Courage rises. Your energy shifts..

In the early years of my career, I was often the only woman in the room. I had to find my way, because many men didn't know how to make room. I learned to contribute without becoming challenging. To be resilient when overlooked. To adapt.

And yet, I rise.

Today, that path is shared with more women than ever. We are rising. We are reshaping. We are rewriting the narrative. We are the roots of change. The food industry needs more women who stand up, speak up, and rise in their own presence.

I wasn't invited to the table. I claimed my place.

So, ask yourself: What part of your voice have you been trimming back just to stay safe? What space could you step into if you stopped apologizing for your presence?

This is my invitation to every woman, whether you're behind the scenes in food production, stocking shelves, managing farm operations, creating a product line from your culinary recipes, cooking in a kitchen of a restaurant, or leading in sales and marketing to take your rightful seat at the table.

You belong. You always have.

This chapter is a seedling from my book, *Authentically Rising: Cultivating Purpose, Presence, and a Seat at the Table*. I hope you'll join me in its pages.

So, come. Take your place.
Here, let me pull out a chair for you.

Cynthia Haskins is a writer, speaker, and artist with four decades of leadership in the fresh produce industry. Known for her grounded wisdom, she inspires women to rise with purpose and presence—championing their growth, strengthening their confidence, and encouraging them to embrace lives of deeper meaning, clarity, and wholeness.

cynthiahaskins.com

Join me for a free one-year membership as we cultivate a network of women rising together with authenticity and purpose. Side by side, we'll learn, lead, and lift each other as we discover new possibilities and take our rightful seat at the table.

Visit CynthiaHaskins.com to join today.

STAYING SANE WHEN YOUR WORLD GOES CRAZY

Rhetah Kwan

> *Love is the bridge between you and everything.*
>
> *—Rumi*

The surgeon appeared from across the room and walked toward me, devoid of any reassuring expression. I was startled, as I expected him to be wearing surgical greens. Instead, he was dressed in a deep blue velvet suit, and he smelled like a perfume factory.

Time seemed to slow, and my emotions teetered between dread and hope. I held my breath, as I struggled to maintain composure. Instead of sitting down next to me, or showing any compassion, he stood looking down on me and said, "He is okay and in recovery."

Relief flooded me—until he confessed it was the toughest gallbladder surgery in his forty-year career, complete with grisly details. My chest tightened. I wanted to scream and race to David's side, desperate for the reassurance that he'd heal, that we would move forward with our lives.

Listening to the surgeon, it occurred to me that it was Valentine's Day, and he likely was late for a date with his wife since the surgery had stretched from two hours to five. The thought flashed through my mind, *What else had he rushed?*

As quickly as he appeared, he was gone, leaving me alone with the scary puzzle pieces of information to sort through while I waited to see David. Restless as a caged tiger, I paced the corridor, desperately praying for calm when I saw a tall, white-haired woman in a long white garment carrying a harp on the escalator, rising like an angel. I felt my mind split; this was so surreal. My body froze in awe and fear, and I heard myself cry out, "Is David dying?" as tears streamed down my face and I sank to my knees.

"Oh, my dear, please let me help you," the woman said kindly. I stared up at her deep-blue eyes and red lipstick as she held out a hand to me. Hesitating, still not knowing if she was really there, I finally took her hand, and she helped me up. We stood gazing into each other's eyes for many minutes.

"Dear one, how can I help?" she asked.

My voice felt hoarse and scratchy as I half-sobbed and told her what the surgeon shared with me, and I described my fears.

"Breathe," she said, placing a hand on my shoulder.

In that moment, I noticed my breaths were shallow, so I shifted to long, deep inhales and exhales to ground myself.

"I have come here to celebrate Valentine's Day and play for people who have loved ones going through surgery." Then she reached into the pocket of her robe and pulled out some chocolate Hershey Kisses and offered me some.

"Everything is better with chocolate," she said, smiling at me.

I looked at her hand and said with a nervous laugh, "Oh yes, Valentine's Day. When I saw you, I thought you were an angel and that . . ."

She stopped me mid-sentence. "That your loved one had crossed over?" she asked. "Yes, I get that reaction a lot." She gave me a hug, picked up her harp, and looked for a place she could start playing.

Feeling numb, I stumbled to a chair across the room from her. I closed my eyes and tried to clear my mind and calm my emotions. I listened to the transformative sounds flowing from the woman's harp. I'm not sure how much time passed, but then a memory of how David and I met appeared in my mind.

My dear friend Michael introduced David to me by bringing him to one of my macrobiotic food potlucks.

When Michael and David showed up, I was in the kitchen cooking a large pot of vegetable and hijiki seaweed soup. I was stirring the soup when Michael bounced into the kitchen with David in tow and announced it was high time we met! David stepped forward, investigated the pot of soup, and commented that it appeared to have little black worms floating around in it.

Then, without looking at me, he said a curt hello and backed out of the kitchen. Michael ran after him and convinced him to stay, even though his resistance made him appear uncomfortable throughout the evening.

At the end of the gathering, I went into the kitchen to clean up, and David followed me. It felt like he was about to say goodbye, but instead he stood there staring at the ametrine ring I was wearing. Looking up at me, he showed me the exact same ring he had on his finger, except his was the much larger male version of my female ring. We looked at each other and smiled, and at that moment I felt a spark pass between us. Not knowing David was an astrologer and very into the meaning of things, I said, "Sure," when he asked if it was "acceptable" to give him my date, time, and place of birth.

He thanked me for the evening and left. A few moments later Michael asked me what I thought of David. He told me this was the first time in six months that David had accepted his invitation. I told Michael what had passed between us with the rings, and he said he was certain this was the beginning of a special relationship.

The following month, I called David to invite him to our next gathering. After a long pause, he said, "No, what I would like is to come over in the afternoon and talk with you, if that is okay?"

"Of course, I would love that," I said, feeling giddy.

The day of the event I was making calendula herbal salve as gifts for everyone. Sensing the beeswax I was using for the base, a few bees flew into the kitchen. I ran around ushering them out and closed the windows as I had no screens.

The doorbell rang, and I went to the door, my heart pounding as David's sparkling blue eyes greeted me. I led him into the kitchen for tea, where he stood quietly with a gentle smile. We ended up talking for hours about spirituality, prayer, meditation, movies, music, art, and what he called the importance of being able to "just be." At that moment we both noticed the bees that had completely covered the outside of the windows, and we laughed until we cried.

He asked me out for dinner and a movie on Friday, and soon it became our sacred ritual, sharing sizzling rice soup at our favorite café, then crossing the street hand in hand to melt into the magic of the movies.

Wednesday afternoon was another favorite escape; we would go swimming in the nearby rivers or ocean waves to refresh our spirits. After each adventure, David would ask me to close my eyes, and then he'd share ancient tales of a "grace-filled life," ending each story by placing a gold ring, a book, a pair of earrings, a poem, or a crystal in my hand. In those moments, I felt childlike wonder as his magical lessons taught me to forgive, love deeply, and let go.

We grew together like two trees in the forest. In his presence, I found a haven, a space where my heart could rest, trust, and rejuvenate. At the time, no one knew except me that he rescued me from the private darkness that threatened to engulf me.

Now it was my turn to rescue him, or so I thought.

I was startled out of my daydream by the nurse telling me to bring the car to the front of the hospital as David was ready to go home.

Leaping up, I felt a bit dizzy and disoriented, and I struggled to remember how to find our car. I could see the nurse and David in a wheelchair waiting for me as I pulled up. Gingerly we helped him into the car, while my mind tried to figure out the best route home. It was now 5:00 p.m. in Santa Monica, California, on a Friday night—and Valentine's Day made the traffic heavier than usual.

The next morning, I ventured out to gather the freshest vegetables and proteins for David, only to return and find him feverish and weak in bed. My heart lurched, and I quickly called his surgeon. He urged me to bring him straight back to the hospital.

It was a blur after that—test after test after test and endless specialists, while David's condition spiraled down each day. The days turned into months, then years, and what followed was a relentless battle against the unknown, as his health deteriorated into a place of shadow and despair. I was shattered as I watched the man I loved retreat into his own mind, his light dimming with each passing day. My desperation consumed me, and I spent every waking moment contacting healers and specialists from all over the globe, asking if they could help or knew anyone who might be able to help.

This was uncharted territory. I had always been the rock for everyone—Mother Support who could always find a way to help. The stabbing pain of feeling helpless was shredding me. Tears flowed endlessly, and my own strength wavered under the weight of it all.

How could this be happening to such a kind, loving, spiritual man? I prayed and begged for answers until I felt I was losing my mind. This shook me on a deep level as I feared that without clarity, I wouldn't be able to care for David.

I forced myself to take gentle breaths, eat wholesome meals, and indulge in restorative catnaps to combat the sleepless nights. In those quiet spaces, a clear insight arose: To truly be with David, I had to open myself to the love and light that was always there and learn to trust again, no matter how impossible this felt.

The ongoing self-realizations from my meditations showed me my shadow, the part of myself normally only seen through others' eyes. My focus was to help David, who appeared to be suffering. Yet, as I reflected on the past eight years, I had to admit that nothing I did made a difference for David. He wasn't asking for help. I was the one who saw him as suffering and kept telling myself I had to help him.

I learned that I couldn't handle seeing him in this state and thus projected the idea that he was suffering when there was no way I could really know this. He wasn't talking or communicating with me in any way. Then it hit me: It was *me*—I was suffering. I was trying to protect myself as it was too hard and way too painful.

Once I allowed myself to accept this, it was easier to begin to shift my perspective. I could hold David in deep love and compassion, instead of responding from a place of terror-fueled urgency. I was able to accept help from a few friends and family members and the wellness community I'd spent eight years building. I arranged for others to deliver nourishing, organic meals along with organic groceries, people to read to David, share music, and even bring a gentle dog for comfort. In that loving release, I honored my own healing to do what I wanted, and I trusted David's journey.

I am forever grateful to my extraordinary wellness community because the steady flow of financial support they generated as independent associates allowed me to secure the highest quality of care for David, even when his care costs soared into the tens of thousands each month, and this gave me the space to be with him.

It is so freeing and honoring that my business partners and I are not bound by titles or paychecks; instead, we have a shared mission to uplift one another in health and in life. Looking back, I was able to stay sane, stay connected to my heart, and make the critical decisions for David's care and my own well-being while our lives were in chaos.

My beautiful David crossed the veil four years ago, and I still feel his gentle smile in every sunrise, every compassionate gesture, and every breath I take on this healing journey. His courage taught me that to care for another, I must first nurture my heart and honor my Soul—and in doing so, find peace.

Today, I carry his light beyond limits, trusting that love endures, transforms, and blossoms in the Soul that remains. Loving, trusting, and connecting with your tribe is the way through. Love brings compassionate insights along the path, and light is always there to guide. If this feels impossible right now, love who and what you can, and don't forget yourself.

What I have learned is to be open to love however it manifests and heals. Whether you can feel it, see it, or know it in any form, it is always there waiting to be invited in. Listen closely—it is calling to all of us . . . and you don't have to do it alone.

Rhetah Kwan is a bestselling author, global entrepreneur, and Certified Life and Wellness Strategist specializing in natural, regenerative light technology. With heart-centered compassion and twenty-one years spent building a vibrant wellness community, she empowers midlife professionals to transform exhaustion into vitality, using proven holistic methods to ignite healing, hope, and limitless financial possibilities.

rhetahkwan.com

Ready to experience vital health and fully engage in your life again? Go to rhetahkwan.com to book your free consultation and discover how regenerative light therapy and community support can transform your life.

CULTIVATING RESILIENCE—LETTING GO, LETTING IN, RISING STRONG

Karen Strauss

Dogs don't dwell in despair—they shake it off, find the next patch of sunshine, and keep going.

One of the greatest lessons I've learned about resilience came from my dog: the ability to move through pain without losing hope. Dogs fall, fail, get sick, get scared—but they don't stay there. They rest, recover, and return with their tails wagging. I didn't know it yet, but I was about to learn the same lesson in a much harder way.

Barely glancing at me, the technician told me to go back to the waiting room—they needed to get more pictures. When you've had as many mammograms as I have, you know exactly what that means.

I sat. And waited. Then sat some more. My body was frozen, but inside, I was unraveling. My mind raced: *What if it's bad? What if I can't handle it? What happens to my business? My life?* I kept going up to the front desk like a child who just needed someone to say it would be okay, asking when they would call me back. I waited another thirty minutes, and finally I felt like I couldn't breathe—my adrenaline was pumping, and I thought I was going to faint. But still no one said anything. And still I waited.

So, I did what I thought would help me feel in control: I ran.

I ran through the double doors and out into the sun-drenched July street, irrationally hoping that if I didn't hear the words, they wouldn't be real. I hopped on the bus and buried myself in the idea that this wasn't happening. I couldn't wait to get home so I could put my head under the covers, irrationally thinking that if the words weren't spoken, I wouldn't have the dreaded "c" word.

But the phone didn't stop ringing.

By the time I got home, there were several urgent messages from the lab telling me I needed to come back immediately.

I made the appointment for the next morning at 8:00 a.m. Then I called my best friend Susan. She dropped everything—she listened to me, grounded me, and insisted on coming with me. Susan isn't just my best friend—she's a women's health provider who knew her way around a radiology room. She held my hand, literally and figuratively, as they confirmed what I already knew deep down.

I had breast cancer.

The bad news: It had started to spread outside the duct. The good news: It was small and caught early.

We walked home in silence, Susan's hand in mine. She said something I'll never forget:

"You're going to be fine. It'll be a rough road for a while, but you'll be just fine. This will become a bump in the road."

But I'm not going to lie: At that moment, it felt like a mountain. It felt like much more than a bump in the road during that long, dreadful year, but during that time I realized how many amazing friends and supporters I had.

For most of my life, I had prided myself on being completely independent. I was the one people came to when they needed support. I ran my own company. I juggled client meetings, teams, deadlines, properties, dogs, and decisions. I didn't ask for help—not because no one was offering, but because I believed needing help meant I wasn't strong.

And now? I was trying to add "manage cancer" to my to-do list.

This was just one more thing ... right?

Well, I couldn't have been more wrong! I didn't realize what a big deal this was, and I needed to focus every bit of attention on getting well—from choosing the surgeon, the oncologist, and getting second and third opinions to finally undergoing the surgery, enduring more endless tests, and setting up the chemo treatment. And then living with the effects of the chemo itself—the nausea, the fatigue, the memory loss ...

Throughout this process, I don't know how I would have made it through without my family, good friends—and surprisingly even those that weren't such good friends.

For instance, one person (now an Oscar winner for the movie *Birdland*!) who I knew from the dog park called me and offered to take my dog Izzy to the park anytime I wanted. I didn't know him very well at that point, and his generous offer floored me.

Similar offers came. A woman in my building is a makeup artist, and when I had a swanky holiday party to attend, she offered to do my makeup—complete with false eyelashes!

And one night, when I decided it was time to cut the remaining hair on my head (a very emotional decision for me), my friend (whose husband works on Broadway) brought over one of her friends who cut hair professionally for Broadway productions. They made it fun—we had champagne and hors d'oeuvres.

One neighbor, who I knew just to say hello to, came to my apartment every night while I was going through chemo to check on me, see if I needed anything, and offer to walk Izzy. This was a lifesaver, since by then I was pretty wiped out and sometimes couldn't even make it off the couch, let alone get dressed in five layers, dress Izzy, and walk in 10 degree weather so Izzy could do his business.

I could go on and on about the generosity and support offered to me by friends, family, and acquaintances who were ready and willing to do something, anything, to help me. And for the first time in my life, I let them! Wow! What a feeling—I went from feeling guilty to feeling grateful and appreciative of the fact that so many people wanted to support and help me. All I had to do was say yes and give them a task.

So many people came to sit with me during the four hours each week I had my chemo treatment. My friends who thought they were stand-up comedians practiced on me, their captive audience. Some of my friends came to gossip, or spill their problems, or just discuss world events. I was SO grateful not to have to talk about "how I was feeling" or about my illness in general. It made the time fly by.

I have never forgotten this lesson. I no longer want to be a loner, to have to make decisions by myself, to not allow myself to be vulnerable. This has stood me in good stead to grow my business as well as become more intimate in my personal relationships.

The Inner Work

In the months that followed—through the surgery, the healing, the exhaustion—I began exploring ways to calm my anxious mind. I discovered a movement practice called Gyrotonic, which helped me regain physical strength and flexibility. I learned about meditation and breathing techniques that helped slow the spiral of fear. I stopped racing forward and started breathing into the now.

And somewhere along the way, deeper questions surfaced: What am I really here to do? What did I want my impact in the world to be—not just in business, but in the lives of others?

Those questions became a turning point.

I realized I wanted to help women amplify their voices. I wanted them to be seen and heard—not "someday," not "when they were ready," but *now*.

I wanted to help the ones with powerful messages stop being the best-kept secret in their industries.

To teach them that writing a book can be the boldest declaration of identity and purpose.

To show them that when you share your story, you become a magnet for opportunity—stages, media, clients, legacy.

That's when it clicked:

This was why I had to heal.

This was why I had to lead.

This was why I had to rise.

What Resilience Really Looks Like

We often think resilience means muscling through. Keeping the mask on. Managing it all and pretending we're fine. But true resilience—the kind that lasts—isn't about never failing. It's about getting back up, asking for help, allowing others to carry you, and staying open to being changed by the experience.

Here's what I know now:

- You can't always go it alone. And you don't have to.
- Letting people walk beside you isn't weakness—it's wisdom.
- Life keeps "lifing," as I like to say. There will be challenges, heartbreaks, disappointments. But also—support, miracles, laughter, transformation.

Resilience is about trusting that even when things fall apart, you don't have to. You may not come back the same, but if you let it, you'll come back stronger, more focused, and more grounded in your purpose.

If you're going through something hard—personally or professionally—I want you to hear this:

- You don't need to have it all figured out.
- You don't need to be perfect.
- You just need to stay in the game.

Let people in. Let go of the myth that strength means doing it all yourself. You'll be amazed by how strong you become when you stop trying to do it alone.

Resilience isn't resistance. It's surrender, support, and the choice to rise again—wiser, bolder, and more open than before.

I've learned that life is more fun when I let people in. I no longer feel the weight of the world on my shoulders. I even hired a business coach to grow my business to the next level. This requires that I share what's going on with me and then listen to her words and know they're without judgment. Her first words to me are always "What do you need?" I know I have mentors, friends, advisors, and loved ones who will keep me grounded, supported, and constantly aware that I do not have to go through life alone.

Dogs know this. They teach us that resilience isn't about pretending everything is fine, it's about leaning into the people who love us, accepting the help, and trusting that joy will return. That's exactly what I did. Like my dog, I eventually stood back up, more focused, stronger, and ready to face the world again—with a little help from my pack.

Karen Strauss has worked in publishing for more than thirty-five years. She is a master book publisher, speaker, book coach, and author. Her company, Hybrid Global Publishing, works with speakers, coaches, authors, and entrepreneurs to write, publish, distribute, and promote their books in order to generate unlimited leads, get on more speaking stages, and grow their business by attracting more clients.

hybridglobalpublishing.com

Scan this QR code for a free gift from Karen!

MISDIAGNOSIS

Karen J.C. Sullivan, PhD
By all rights, I should be dead.

On Saturday, January 20, 1990, I was shopping in a small, family-owned store with my mother, browsing through crafts, fabrics, and other items as we often did on Saturdays after our morning workout. Suddenly, I was overcome with an intense pain in my left leg. I have a high pain tolerance, but the intensity of the sensation I was feeling was all-consuming.

Earlier that morning, I spent an hour doing weight training, followed by ninety minutes of high-impact aerobics, and then a whirlpool soak. I hadn't experienced any pain or discomfort during or after all of those activities.

I told my mother that something was very wrong with my leg, and when she saw my face, she quickly asked if I wanted to go to the emergency room. I told her no; I just wanted to get home and put my leg up so I could try to figure out what was going on.

We had taken my car, so I dropped my mother off and made it home without difficulty. Fortunately, I wasn't driving a car with a stick shift, because the pain in my left leg was increasing, and it was becoming immovable. Getting out of the car was difficult, and I noticed that while my movement didn't change the pain, its intensity never wavered.

Once out of the car, I looked up at my cute little townhouse, the first home I had ever purchased. It was an accomplishment I was so proud of, but now it became a place of pain as I crawled up the two flights of stairs to my bedroom. I hoped the pain would subside or lessen after I had time to rest.

The pain continued to increase over the weekend, and on Monday, I contacted my healthcare practitioner, hoping they would have an answer, and more importantly, something to relieve, or at least lessen the intensity of the excruciating, constant pain. Over the weekend, my husband had been home, tending to me and bringing me food, but he had just started a new job, so he had to leave for work. My mother met me at the bottom of the stairs and helped me outside to her car so she could drive me to the doctor's office.

Once in the examination room, the practitioner assessed my leg. They said there was no redness, no swelling, and they told me that my left leg, which felt huge to me, was the same temperature as my right leg. They concluded that I did not have a blood clot. They explained that a blood clot would cause redness, warmth, and swelling, and often have a red streak down the leg.

When the health practitioner asked about my activities, I explained that I taught a high-intensity aerobic dance class four times a week. The practitioner diagnosed a torn ligament based on my history of dancing and working out in other athletic activities, prescribed ibuprofen and Percocet, which is a narcotic, both to be taken as needed over the next few days, and advised me to walk around as much as I could tolerate so as not to have my leg stiffen and swell, which would happen if I were too sedentary. Walking would allow my leg to maintain some range of motion. To my fitness instructor's ear, what they diagnosed and advised makes sense—at least it did on Monday.

On the way home from the doctor's office, my mother stopped at the drugstore, filled my prescriptions, and then took me home. At my house, she fixed me something to eat, and then I once again crawled up the two flights of stairs on my hands and knees, dragging my left leg with my arm. Once in my bedroom, I slowly changed my clothes and fell onto the bed.

That week, my husband left early in the morning and came home in the early evening, always coming upstairs right away to check on me. Every morning, he would go downstairs and prepare something for me to eat for breakfast and lunch, as well as something to drink, and he would put it in our little red-and-white mini cooler. I would remain in bed in pain.

On Monday and Tuesday, I tried to move my leg, but I quickly knew "walking around" was impossible. The pain was excruciating and only continued to increase. Every night, I twisted and turned and cried. By Thursday, I was crying all day as well. I was inconsolable. Neither the ibuprofen nor the Percocet provided any relief. Simply going to the bathroom was a long, painful ordeal, with me crawling or pulling myself to the edge of the bed, sliding down from the bed to the floor, dragging myself with my left leg, pain throbbing, crying all the way. This went on for days.

Finally, after almost a week, I called my healthcare practitioner to give them an update and ask for suggestions and guidance on what I might do to reduce the pain. I spoke to the same practitioner who had seen me on Monday, and they said, "Yeah, these injuries take a long time to heal." Even though I told them the medication was not providing any relief, they encouraged me to continue taking the medication around the clock to "get on top of the pain."

Over the next two days, I took the medication as the doctor told me, but it still didn't touch my pain, and I finally stopped taking it. I wasn't eating much, I wasn't sleeping, and as I lay in bed, I remember thinking that I couldn't continue to live with this intensity of pain. I knew it had to be more than a torn ligament.

My husband spent the evenings with me, but he had to sleep in another room because my crying and writhing around kept him awake, and a lack of sleep would have a negative impact on his performance at his new job.

During the many hours of pain, I sought comfort by reciting the Twenty-Third Psalm, over and over and over again, almost nonstop. After several days, I was sure I was dying. Feeling a sense of peace and calm, I left my body. I remember looking down on the bed, seeing myself lying still on the bed, my eyes closed, no longer writhing in pain, and I heard God speak to me. He told me, "It's not your time, Karen; I have work for you to do. You're not dying. You're not going to die. It's not your time." Then I was back in my body, looking up, fully aware, and feeling calmer; my crying subsided for a little while.

After another ten days with no relief, I called the doctor's office and asked to speak to a different practitioner, the primary physician in charge of that office. I told them the pain hadn't decreased and that the medication had no impact on the pain. That doctor said, "This has been going on too long without improvement. I want to see you in my office today; we've got to figure out what is going on and get some relief for you." I was relieved and grateful to hear those words!

My mother once again took me to the doctor's office. My leg was still not red, it wasn't hot, it wasn't swollen, and it was hard to distinguish the difference between my left leg and my right leg. By now, I was using a cane to avoid the extra surge of pain felt when I put weight on my left leg. When we arrived at the doctor's office, my mother pulled up to the door and went inside to get someone to help me out of the car. A nurse helped me into a wheelchair and wheeled me into the doctor's office, my mother following close behind.

The doctor greeted us, concern evident in their facial expression. This doctor knew me well—my family had been going to this practice for many years. They knew I was a nurse; they knew I was stoic. My presentation was unlike anything they'd ever seen before, and I could see how concerned they were. The practitioner examined my left leg using a Doppler ultrasound, showed me the screen, and said, "There's no blood flowing here—you have a deep vein thrombosis, and you must go to the hospital. I'm calling an ambulance, and you'll go there immediately. This is a medical emergency!'

I felt relief and anger, relief to have a diagnosis, but anger that it had taken so long and that the misdiagnosis could have, by all rights, cost me my life. As a nurse, I knew that I should have been dead. The worst thing to tell a patient with a deep vein thrombosis (DVT) is to walk on the leg. The chances of dying from that are significant, and that misdiagnosis almost cost me my life.

I went to the hospital by an ambulance, sirens blaring, lights flashing. Once I arrived at the hospital emergency room, a nurse quickly inserted an IV into my arm, and within minutes, I was taken upstairs to a patient room and admitted. I was restricted to bed rest with bathroom privileges, which meant I was only allowed to get out of bed with my IV pole and walk a couple of feet to the bathroom and back to bed. Period.

A few days after being admitted to the hospital, I was discharged and put on Heparin, a blood thinner, which I had to inject into my abdomen every day, three times a day. I was on Heparin for the entire pregnancy and wore a medical alert bracelet to inform anyone treating me medically that, should I be unable to speak, I was on a blood thinner.

I returned to the practitioner who had correctly diagnosed my DVT for a follow-up visit. They advised me that I would have to elevate my legs every day from now on—at least once, but preferably twice a day—for twenty minutes to help lessen the swelling that had developed from the blood clot.

The two weeks the blood clot was misdiagnosed cost me. The damage to the vein was significant; the blood flow down my leg and back up to my heart had been slowed. My practitioner prescribed a permanent handicap disability placard and told me I would need that for the rest of my life, because the damage to my leg was going to continue to cause swelling. My leg was sore, and they didn't know if that soreness would go away or not.

So I left the doctor's office with the diagnosis of venous insufficiency, pain that affected my ability to walk, and a prescription for a permanent handicap placard in my hand. Oh, and what I didn't mention yet is that at the time, I was ten weeks pregnant!

When I was finally able to go back to work, I often shared this story of strength, overcoming, and perseverance with those who also faced serious medical issues.

Important Takeaways

- When speaking with a healthcare provider, make sure your concerns are heard and addressed.
- When you sense something is wrong, write down the symptoms, your concerns, and any questions you have for the practitioner.
- Do not leave the doctor's office until all your questions and concerns have been addressed and resolved.

- Be sure you receive a copy of the Patient's Rights and read it in its entirety.
- Take a loved one or friend with you to medical appointments for serious issues; having another person to hear what the practitioner says is very helpful, as it is easy to miss important information when you are distressed or in pain.

While I wouldn't wish what I went through on anyone, I am grateful every day to be alive. The resilience and inner strength I developed have allowed me to help others overcome their suffering.

Karen J.C. Sullivan, PhD, is a strengths-finder who empowers highly educated Black women to recognize their true power and overcome self-doubt. Through coaching, writing, and speaking, Dr. Karen helps people explore their past to create their future, turning tragedies into triumphs and finding their buried treasure.

linkedin.com/in/karenjcumberbatchsullivan/

FINDING MY VOICE

Claudia Volkman

What if you lost your voice—and it never came back?

Years ago, I got my start in publishing working at Tyndale House Publishers in Wheaton, Illinois. The founder, Dr. Kenneth Taylor, was a visionary and the creator of The Living Bible, a paraphrase of Scripture that has sold more than 40 million copies. While he was getting close to completing the last books of The Living Bible, he started to lose his voice, which he writes about in a chapter of his autobiography called "Voice Problems." He consulted doctors and tried all kinds of lozenges, sprays, and other remedies. He even visited faith healers, but to no avail. Finally a Jewish psychiatrist suggested that his laryngitis might be the result of subconscious guilt for "tampering with the Word of God." Whatever the cause, Dr. Taylor never regained his voice and always spoke in a gravelly whisper.

Most of us, I'm guessing, take our voices for granted. Many of us don't like the sound of our own voices either. That's because our voices sound different when we hear recordings. But having a voice is a gift. It gives us the ability to express who we are, share our stories, stand up for what matters, and connect deeply with others. With our words, we can comfort, inspire, challenge, or heal. And just think if your ability to speak was suddenly taken away or diminished. Instead of being critical of the way you sound, see your voice as something to be grateful for.

It takes a while to find your voice—at least that's been true in my case. I'm what you might call a "late bloomer" ... which actually has served me well now that I'm in my seventies (young at heart! Still blooming!). I was the only child of two introverts, so our house was pretty quiet. I lived in the world of books and art, surrounded by my large collection of stuffed animals and my imagination. I had lots of friends in my neighborhood, all who came from large families, and I loved being part of their noisy, vocal households.

As I grew up, my faith helped me come alive, and I began to come out of my shell. I married the love of my life, had two adorable sons, and was fortunate to be able to be a stay-at-home mom, although I worked as a Montessori assistant directress at the school our boys attended. I was in my early forties when I got my first full-time publishing job at Tyndale House. My role was production coordinator, which meant I had a number of projects that I shepherded through the publishing process—from manufacturing to editorial, design, typesetting, and sales—keeping everything on schedule. This required interacting with a large number of employees (unlike the editors I encountered who were locked away in their solitary offices), and this taught me how to communicate clearly and negotiate deadlines. In other words, while I was learning all aspects of the publishing industry, I also was learning to use my voice. I eventually moved into the special sales department where my title was creative editor, which taught me to express my voice on paper. I went on to work at several other publishing houses, always learning and increasing my skills. I added author acquisitions, product development, and developmental editing to my repertoire.

While I was helping others find their voices in publishing, I was only beginning to discover my own. I loved what I did, but I did it quietly, content to be behind the scenes. Somehow I always felt that others had more expertise, more knowledge, were more articulate ... I was always the learner, never the teacher. Whether in my full-time jobs or in the freelance work I did on the side, I was happy being the silent partner who came alongside others and helped their words to shine, their impact to increase.

When my last full-time publishing job ended in 2018, I knew it was time to step up and launch my own business. Still the creative editor, I called my company Creative Editorial Solutions, and today I provide book coaching, developmental editing, ghostwriting and book doctoring, copyediting, proofreading, and professionally formatted book interiors for authors, entrepreneurs, coaches, and speakers.

And then I began to notice something. Over the years, the authors I served affirmed me in unexpected ways, crediting me with bringing their voices to life in ways they had struggled to do on their own. This began to happen more frequently when Karen Strauss gave me the opportunity to coach authors who needed developmental editing. I helped them formulate their ideas and pull their manuscripts together—and suddenly, the world of author coaching opened up! I found myself feeling energized and inspired after spending thirty to sixty minutes on a Zoom call with an author. And I was amazed the first time I saw someone taking notes during my session with them—were they actually writing down something *I* said?

Only later did I realize that helping others uncover their voices was helping me find mine.

The Author's Voice

In my work as an editor, I always strive to make sure my authors' content stays in their "voice"—I never want to edit out their unique style or tone. Just as each of us has a distinctive voice orally, when you write you have a unique voice too. As an author, your voice is the heartbeat of your writing—it's what makes your work unique, recognizable, and emotionally resonant. Your style and tone are important too, but your voice is the distinct personality that comes through on the page. It's shaped by your perspective, values, word choices, flow, and the way you see the world.

Your voice is how readers come to know and trust you. A strong voice builds connection and credibility. It goes beyond merely absorbing information; it allows readers to feel like they're having a conversation with you. It can make them feel like you understand their pain, and it can inspire them to overcome challenges. While getting the facts right is important, readers are looking for more than facts; they're looking for solutions from a trusted source they can believe in, learn from, and relate to.

Whether you're sharing a personal story, offering expert advice, or writing to motivate and empower, a compelling voice is what keeps readers engaged and makes your message memorable—different from all the other books written on the same topic. Having an authentic voice allows you to communicate with clarity and impact—and this especially important when you're writing about emotional or transformative topics.

Whether you're writing a book or living your best life, here are four tips for finding and refining your voice:

1. **Pay Attention to What Moves You**

   What stirs your emotions? What are you curious about? What compels you to speak up? What are you passionate about? What unique experiences have shaped your worldview? When you write or speak from those places, your voice naturally becomes more authentic and compelling.

2. **Embrace Your Quirkiness**

Don't try to hide or suppress your natural rhythm, humor, perspective, or even your imperfections—especially your imperfections. Your individuality—your word choices, how you see the world, the way you tell a story—is your greatest asset. The more you embrace what makes you you, the stronger and more memorable your voice becomes.

3. **Write (or Speak) the Way You Talk to a Trusted Friend**

    Sometimes we fall into the trap of feeling like we have to be something other than ourselves, something more than "just us." But if you try too hard to sound "professional" or "inspirational," your real voice can get lost. Think of the way you express yourself with your friends; your words naturally carry warmth and honesty. These are the hallmarks of an authentic voice.

4. **Notice What You *Don't* Want to Sound Like**

    Clarity often comes through contrast. Pay attention to writing that feels forced, flat, or disconnected—and ask yourself why. Notice how talking with some people makes you feel lighter, inspired, or engaged, while others leave you feeling drained and tired. Recognizing what doesn't resonate with you will help you define what *does*.

Like I said, I'm a late bloomer. In many ways, I'm still finding my voice and experimenting with new ways of using it all the time. I'm not always as articulate as I aspire to be, and that's OK. But the more I practice—whether writing, speaking, coaching, or just having meaningful conversations with others, the more my confidence grows. It's the same for all of us—we're always becoming more of who we really are. Our beliefs, convictions, emotions, and truth will continue to evolve as long as we're alive.

Finding your voice takes honesty, self-awareness, and practice. Whether you're crafting a memoir or navigating a major life decision, your voice is your compass. And when you find it, you stop asking for permission to speak or live fully—you simply *do*. The more you honor your voice, the more powerful your stories become—on the page and in the world.

Claudia Volkman has more than thirty-five years of experience in the publishing industry. Now, as the owner of Creative Editorial Solutions, she assists publishers, authors, entrepreneurs, and speakers with their editorial needs. Services include book coaching, developmental editing, book doctoring, copyediting, proofreading, and creating book interiors. A Chicago native, Claudia resides in Southwest Florida.

claudiavolkman.com

To get your free report, "Five Reasons Every Author Needs an Editor," visit claudiavolkman.com.

BEYOND THE PINK: AWAKENING AND ARISING TO A NEW PARADIGM

Beverly Vote

Without vision, the people perish.

—*Proverbs 29:18*

I didn't ask for a dream that would change the course of my life, and I certainly didn't ask for breast cancer. But both came. And both have shaped my right to rise.

It was August 8, 2008, when I had the dream that shattered me open in a holy way. In that dream, I was shown that we, as a planet and as individuals, have no vision for the end of breast cancer. We have awareness campaigns, research studies, treatment centers, pink promises, and pink everything, but what we don't have is a vision for a world beyond the disease. That realization hit me like a spiritual lightning bolt.

It made me realize how we have normalized breast cancer. How we've built entire industries, identities, and expectations around surviving, but not transcending. That dream confirmed that we have put more faith in the next pharmaceutical discovery than we have in the healing power of prayer. Rarely, if at all, is this discussed in many breast cancer communities or groups. We ask others to pray for us and for one another, but how focused are we on earnestly praying for the global end of breast cancer?

But I need to take you back before the dream, back to when I was just trying to survive my own diagnosis. I was thirty-eight when I heard the words no one ever wants to hear. The diagnosis came a year after being misdiagnosed four times. It was a bleak diagnosis, and my doctor at the time didn't provide enough encouragement or hope other than the possibility of future clinical trials. Inside I was screaming, *How does that help me now? Is that all you have for me?*

What followed were eight years of hell: surgeries, treatments, and a whirlwind of fear, doubt, and a gnawing sense of survivor's guilt, not to mention what my family went through. I wondered constantly: *Why am I still here? What's the point of my life now? Will this nightmare ever be over?*

For years, I wandered in the fog of those questions, afraid to fully live because I was caught up in all the "unknowns and what ifs" of what might happen next. It wasn't until I wrote a life mission statement that things began to shift. I didn't even know if it would matter, but I needed something to move me out of that fog. I wrote:

"My life mission is to help change the culture and consciousness of breast cancer."

That statement gave my pain a purpose. I poured myself obsessively into learning all I could. I sought a way to make a difference, and that led to starting the *Breast Cancer Wellness Magazine* in 2006. In the process, I connected with survivors and supporters across the country. But the dream I had in 2008 took it all deeper. It forced me to look at breast cancer differently, to explore the concept of healing more deeply, and to experience prayer differently and more profoundly than I had previously understood.

The more I paid attention, the more I began to see how the dominant narrative around breast cancer keeps us disconnected from our inner wisdom and God's higher-healing power. I began to see the disease differently through an energetic, emotional, and spiritual lens.

All of which kept raising more questions:

What if it is true that faith the size of a mustard seed is more powerful than human expectation?

What if it is true that people perish where there is no vision?

What if it is true that one of the greatest gifts to heal our lives and to heal our planet is the power of prayer?

What if Faith Believers from around the world were to pray for the end of breast cancer—how powerful would that be?

What if breast cancer is a catalyst, one that compels us to think differently—radically differently?

What if it's not just a medical crisis, but a spiritual and cultural crisis, one that invites us to question everything we've believed about healing, identity, and what it means to truly be more vibrantly alive and to be transformed from victim to victor? Maybe it's not here to break us, but to break open the old paradigm . . . so we can rise into a new one: The New Pink Paradigm™, where vision, faith, and our soul-aligned strength reshape what's possible after diagnosis.

What if there is a greater paradigm for us to rise into, one that goes beyond what we can currently conceive and that defies medical prognosis odds?

What if the answers to end breast cancer don't come from those whose careers, livelihoods, and investments are in the breast cancer industry but from a driving force elsewhere?

Answering those questions wasn't instantaneous, and it certainly wasn't easy. I had to overcome my own doubts and disbeliefs, overwhelming fear, the silence of shame, and the invisible grip of survivor's guilt. There were days I questioned my worth, my purpose, and why I was still here when others were not. I had to face the unspoken truth I carried: that I had abandoned myself by living by everyone else's expectations.

To rise meant I had to change my beliefs and opinions and open my eyes what was possible beyond society's current narratives. I had to unlearn the belief that healing was only about the body. I had to confront the pink ribbon narratives that comforted some but confined me. And I had to lean more deeply into faith. Not a faith based on formulas, but a living, breathing trust in the idea that prayer could transform not just disease but my way of life.

Rising meant surrendering to a new vision. It meant letting go of what was familiar but broken and stepping forward beyond my fears. It meant daring to believe that my voice and the dream on 08-08-08 could help others rise too. But this Bible verse reminds me and assures me that breast cancer survivors are capable of far greater experiences than we often believe possible:

> *Now to him who is able to do immeasurably more*
> *than all we ask or imagine, according to his power*
> *that is at work within us ...*
> —Ephesians 3:20, NIV

That power is already within us. Our healing. Our rising. Our vision. And our divine capacity to call forth a world where breast cancer no longer defines who we are.

Nearly two decades ago, I founded the Breast Cancer Thrivers Cruise with a simple, radical intention: to celebrate. Not to wait until someone was "cancer-free." But to honor life now, in all its messiness, milestones, and magic. Celebration, I believe, is not a luxury in healing. It is a necessity. It reminds us that joy is not only possible after trauma; it is proof we are still alive.

Now entering its twentieth year, the Breast Cancer Thrivers Cruise is the longest-running cruise event in the world dedicated to breast cancer survivors and supporters. We've celebrated birthdays, held memorials at sea, danced, laughed and cried together, and made lifelong friends who understand what it means to be devasted and overwhelmed, yet still rise. Our 2026 sailing will be our most meaningful sailing yet: "Anchors of Hope: A Global Celebration of Strength and Solidarity." This isn't just another trip. It's a landmark journey for every soul who dares to live, love, and celebrate out loud. Because healing doesn't just happen in hospitals or holistic centers—it happens when we come together and breathe in the essence of vitality.

That rising continued, hard-earned and God-led, and became the foundation for what would eventually emerge as The New Pink Paradigm™, a prayer-powered global vision born from the dream that we are meant to heal more fully, live more boldly, and believe in something far greater than our current circumstance . . . and that it begins with vision, faith, and prayer.

Truth and Transparency > Trust and Transformation

The New Pink Paradigm™ emerged from the core belief that true healing is not solely physical; it is cultural, emotional, spiritual, and global. The New Pink Paradigm™ is not just a movement; it is a healing evolution grounded in the principle that truth and transparency are the gateway to trust and transformation. It's a radical yet proactive reimagining of what becomes possible when we invite something greater into our healing journey. It is not a program or campaign; it's a call to rise. It challenges survivors to release identities rooted in illness and communities to break free from outdated paradigms of care and recovery. This is where faith meets function, where vision overrides fear, and where possibility begins to out-perform prognosis.

Rising into a new reality, for ourselves and for our planet, requires preparation. It means learning to see beyond the symptoms and the systems that have held us back. The global shift we long for will not descend from institutions; it will rise from within each of us. It begins with individuals, survivors, visionaries, and leaders who recognize that a higher consciousness is already breaking through and who choose to become active participants in that shift. The macro (our shared world) reflects the micro (our personal transformation), and the world's healing depends on ours. Every healed belief, every surrendered fear, every courageous declaration that "I was made for more" becomes a ripple in the rising tide that moves us from a story of disease ... to a future shaped by destiny.

Global Prayer Day for the End of Breast Cancer: August 8, 2026

In August of 2026, we will gather across nations, time zones, and beliefs for a singular purpose: to pray for the global end of breast cancer. The New Pink Paradigm Global Prayer Day is scheduled to take place on 08-08-26. More than an event, this is a worldwide call to transcend statistics, treatment plans, and sorrow, and to unite in a shared moment of sacred intention. This isn't about pushing one religion over another; it's about returning to the deep knowing that healing, *true healing*, begins when we collectively ask in unified prayer for something higher, bolder, and more lasting than what medicine alone can offer.

This global gathering is a call to lift both the wounded and the weary. To intercede for every mother in fear, every partner unsure how to help, every child absorbing the weight of diagnosis through whispered tears behind closed doors. We pray for survivors who know in their bones they were born for more than "the breast cancer experience," for physicians constrained by broken systems, and for the silent skeptics who dare not hope because the pain of disappointment cuts too deep. It is time we dared anyway.

The Global Prayer Day is an invitation to all people, regardless of background, to lend their voice, their hope, their faith, or even just their breath to a future where breast cancer no longer defines us. It is our collective turning point, a spiritual uprising wrapped in love and bold enough to believe that this can, in fact, end.

I have risen, not just because I overcame a diagnosis.

I have risen because I said "yes" to a mission greater than my fear.

I have risen because I dared to accept a higher dream for myself, for others, and for this planet.

I have risen because I believe, with all my heart, that we can pray, envision, and move forward with a more clearly defined objective in mind, to create together a world where breast cancer no longer dwells or defines us.

That is my right to rise. And it is yours too.

Beverly Vote is a visionary leader, advocate, and author committed to shifting the culture and consciousness surrounding breast cancer. She is the creator of the *Breast Cancer Wellness Magazine* and the founder of the Breast Cancer Thrivers Cruise. She and her husband of fifty-four years live in Missouri.

yournewpinkparadigm.com

You Were Born to Rise

Whether you are a breast cancer survivor or supporter, your story, your pain, your victories, your faith, matters more than you may realize. The right to rise is not just about standing up after being knocked down; it's about remembering who you truly are and embracing the higher purpose waiting for you.

I invite you to take a gentle yet powerful step forward. Scan the QR code or visit YourNewPinkParadigm.com to join a community of hearts and souls rising together.

Find encouragement and hope from others who understand the journey.

Access healing resources designed to uplift and strengthen your spirit.

Stand with us in unity as we prepare for the Global Prayer Day on 08-08-26, believing in miracles and the end of breast cancer.

The world needs the light you carry. Rise, not just for yourself, but for all who are still finding their way.

Scan the QR code, and let's rise together.

FIRE ON THE FRONT LINES

Revolution versus the Flower Child Mirage
Frances Whitten

> *They're going to come with smiles for you and those jobs.*
> — My Grandmother

It was a Sunday afternoon in August. We're on the front porch after dinner for our weekly family chat and wave to the neighbors who walk by. I was about to head back to college for my senior year after working all summer at my first job. I had gotten a C in genetics the previous semester, and when my mother found out, she informed me that she wanted her money back because she didn't pay for Cs. She let me know that if she didn't get her money back, she would not be paying for my final year of college.

She was not smiling. I got a job.

However, having to get a job was not the most shocking part of that summer. My whole career path changed that Sunday afternoon when someone asked what my plans were after graduation. I blithely announced my plans to go to San Francisco and become a hippie for a while.

Silence.

My grandmother spoke first. "Chile, you ain't got time to go to San Francisco and be no hippie. You better get this education we are trying to buy for you and get a decent job while those crazy children are distracted. They are going to come to their senses soon, and then they are going to come with smiles for you and those jobs."

Which is exactly what happened.

Dreamers and Displacement

The "flower children" left Woodstock and "The Summer of Love"; they eventually aged out of their militancy and their youthful rejection of traditional norms, experiments with drugs, and communal living. They made adjustments to the assignations of JFK, MLK, and MLK. They marveled at the Moon Landing and established Earth Day. While this was happening, the counterculture morphed into the buy-culture. Rock music became Big Business and the rebellion became profitable.

In the real world, LSD and hard drugs were flooding into the Black communities, while Black people had no access to planes and were not crossing borders. White people poured into the Black communities, pretending goodwill and bringing gentrification and placebos. They had two destinations in mind: the community itself and our schools. Thus began the era of gentrification that has continued into the first quarter of the twenty-first century.

Gentrification Arrives

Gentrification is a term coined in 1964 by Ruth Glass. In gentrification, new populations move their middle- and upper-income households into working-class urban neighborhoods, which leads to the renovation of and displacement of original lower-income residents. The focus is on the physical and social transformation of neighborhoods, but the displacement of the working-class changes the social character of the urban district.

In the late 1960s and early 1970s, this was mostly small-scale and individually driven. People bought up homes, renovated them, and shifted neighborhood dynamics subtly but meaningfully. In D.C., after the 1968 assassination of Dr. Martin Luther King Jr., entire corridors were gutted—not just by riots, but by divestment. What followed was a slow but intentional acquisition of Black-owned spaces.

By the twenty-first century, gentrification had become a developer-led machine. It came cloaked in the language of "urban renewal." Communities lost not only homes but cultural landmarks, businesses, and the political influence that came with shared space.

Gentrification now hides behind public policy, tax incentives, zoning loopholes, and real estate jargon. But its effect remains the same: displacement, erasure, and loss.

In my own community, we watched it happen. We had to fight to preserve even one fire station—Station #8—staffed exclusively by Black firefighters since 1918. It took community organizing and education to keep that piece of our history alive.

> *You can't just come in when people have a culture that's been laid down for generations. You come in and shit gotta change because you're here?*
> — *Spike Lee*

Gentrifying the Schools

As the flower children evolved, many drifted into education. And just as they brought their ideals into our neighborhoods, they brought them into our classrooms.

They came to "fix" our schools with M&Ms and Skittles, because apparently, Black children need candy to sit still. They eliminated vocational training that had long provided paths to independence: auto mechanics, carpentry, metal work, business math, typing, drafting, and home economics.

Why were these programs removed? They said it was about changing labor markets. About prioritizing academics. But the result was clear: fewer Black youth could walk out of high school with the skills to get a decent job or start a business. That meant fewer who could fund their own freedom, organize their communities, or challenge systems.

In place of practical education, we got "open classrooms" with wall-less learning, no structure, and no accountability. Teachers were now facilitators. Standards were unclear. Assessments were standardized but detached from what was actually taught.

I once tried to assist a teacher with a totally prepared lesson that contained step-by-step instruction for implementation. She turned and asked me, "Where are the answers?" When I replied, "In my head," she just clicked her teeth and left the lesson my desk.

This is what happens when systems pretend to help Black children.

What Schools Need Now

Education doesn't need more cleverness. It needs clarity.

We need:

- **Critical thinking, adaptability, and emotional intelligence** taught alongside academics.
- **Competency-based learning** that requires mastery before moving on.
- **Digital literacy** beyond gaming—teach coding, data analysis, and media skills.

- **Equitable funding and hiring** to retain teachers who see students fully.
- **Inclusive discipline models** that keep kids learning rather than excluding them.

If we want to prepare students for their future, we can't keep teaching them with methods from our past.

Education is the most powerful weapon, which you can use to change the world.
— *Nelson Mandela*

We need to prepare students for THEIR future, not OUR past.
— *Ian Jukes*

Frances Whitten is a retired chemistry teacher of fifty years. She has taught in varied settings. Beginning in Washington, D.C., and extending to Teheran, Iran, Tokyo, Japan, the Dominican Republic, Virginia, and Georgia. As an educator, Frances is passionate about providing information that acknowledges the value of different points of view. In her abundance of free time, she enjoys baking, the public library, and photography. Frances lives in Virginia with her nieces and their children.

Scan the QR code to receive a free PDF containing three ideas for expanding critical thinking activities in your classroom.

www.ingramcontent.com/pod-product-compliance
Lightning Source LLC
Chambersburg PA
CBHW070156080526
44586CB00015B/2016